C000271660

ASPECTS OF TEESSIDE

Aspects of
TEESSIDE
DISCOVERING LOCAL HISTORY

Edited by
MAUREEN ANDERSON

Series Editor
Brian Elliott

Wharncliffe Books

First Published in 2002 by
Wharncliffe Books
an imprint of
Pen and Sword Books Limited,
47 Church Street, Barnsley,
South Yorkshire. S70 2AS

Copyright © Wharncliffe Books 2002

*For up-to-date information on other titles produced under the
Wharncliffe imprint, please telephone or write to:*

> Wharncliffe Books
> FREEPOST
> 47 Church Street
> Barnsley
> South Yorkshire S70 2BR
> Telephone (24 hours): 01226 - 734555

ISBN: 1-903425-19-0

*All rights reserved. No part of this publication may be
reproduced, stored in a retrieval system, or transmitted, in
any form or by any means, electronic, mechanical,
photocopying, recording or otherwise, without the prior
permission in writing of the publishers.*

*This book is sold subject to the condition that it shall not,
by way of trade or otherwise, be lent, resold, hired out or
otherwise circulated without the publisher's prior consent in
any form of binding or cover other than that in which it is
published and without a similar condition including this
condition being imposed on the subsequent purchaser.*

A CIP catalogue record of this book is available from the
British Library

Cover illustration: The river Tees and Wilton Castle, c.1805 (Peter Davison)

Printed in the United Kingdom by
CPI UK

CONTENTS

INTRODUCTION

by

Maureen Anderson

The general public has developed a keen interest in local and family history over the last few years. Finding out how and where their ancestors lived, worked and played has become a quest for many. Tracing our history is achieved in different ways, archaeologists dig up, and historians dig into, the past, their findings are documented and passed on to archives, museums and libraries. Families do some detective work to find the source of grandad's old photographs and letters. Then there are the historians who have a specialist interest in a particular subject and it becomes a passion to gain as much knowledge as possible in that area. Bring these people together, each one writing about their own pet interests and providing illustrations to compliment the written work and you have a book that has a wide appeal.

Wharncliffe Books has been producing the *Aspects* series since 1993, the first volumes relating to South Yorkshire. The series has proved so popular that many new titles are being published on many other English towns and areas. *Aspects of Teesside* has given the opportunity for historians in our area to have previously unpublished or revised, updated work put into print for a wide readership.

As the book is read, it may bring to mind a train, stopping at totally different stations but all linked by a common denominator, the railway track. Teesside's industrial heritage began with the coming of the railway and many of the contributions are linked through mention of this event and the people who were the prime force and wealth behind the venture, the Quakers.

As with much of Britain, boundaries and titles are, from time to time, altered. Some changes to areas of the North East have been: Yorkshire to County Durham to Teesside to Cleveland to Tees Valley. Very confusing! There is controversy over just what towns and villages belong or belonged to Teesside. To try and clarify this Tom Pailor takes us on a curious journey using different forms of transport, as he defines Teesside and puts to rest any confusion the reader may have had. Or does he? The facts relating to the opening of the S & D Railway, including a light hearted human interest touch, are told to us by Norman Moorsom who has already written many books, especially on his much loved home town of Middlesbrough.

Simon Chapman, who has developed a keen interest in the mining aspects of the area, explains how, not only do county titles change but also place names can alter and the original meaning can be lost in the mists of time.

Gary Green passes on his expertise by sharing his undersea adventure that brought together a series of events that were to record an all too common North Sea tragedy. His story is a strong part of our links to the past, as shipping was once the only means of transporting cargo to and from distant lands.

The contributions would not be complete without the legend of the monkey hanging at Old Hartlepool, 'or is it legend?' Paul Screeton takes us through a story that has lived on and is still the butt of many jokes. He also explains how officialdom can be mocked as a mayor takes his seat of honour for a year. On a more serious note regarding Hartlepool, Brian Arnison writes about a nineteenth century printing firm, Proctors. Printers such as this were the beginnings of the media, as we know it today.

Wars, sadly, are part of our heritage and John Perrin gives us the details of the early warning systems without which, many lives would have been lost and many stories would not have been written.

Teesside would not exist had there had not been a river Tees and from ancient times to the present, this waterway has been the lifeblood of the area. Robert Woodhouse takes us along the river's course from an early shipping route to heavy industry. He also gives us an insight into how the Bishops of Durham lived by investigating the history of the impressive building that once overlooked the river.

Geoff Braddy and Peter Davison also explore ancient history. Geoff takes us to Middlesbrough Priory, occupied by the Benedictine or black monks, who seemed to be continuously arguing over property and ownership while Peter looks at the turbulent history of the family that once occupied Wilton Castle.

In conclusion I would like to thank all at Wharncliffe Books for their support on what for me has been a new and very different venture. My thanks also to all the contributors for their hard work and commitment to produce a very interesting and informative volume.

Anyone interested in making a contribution to a possible second volume of *Aspects of Teesside* should, in the first instance, contact Maureen Anderson, c/o Wharncliffe Books, 47 Church Street, Barnsley, S70 2AS.

Please include a working title and an approximate 300 word summary.

1. 'TEESSIDE': A CURIOUS JOURNEY

by Tom Pailor

In fitness for the urgent hour
Unlimited, untiring power
Steam, mighty steam, ascends the throne
And reigns Lord Paramount alone.
William Harrison, nineteenth century engineer.

MUCH DISCUSSION HAS TAKEN PLACE ABOUT the 'City of Teesside' concept, recently described in the *Gazette* as encompassing Stockton, Middlesbrough, Redcar and Cleveland. Many new official bodies have now acquired the grand 'Tees Valley' title, but where exactly is Teesside?

In April 1968 the County Borough of Teesside was founded and incorporated Middlesbrough, Thornaby, Stockton, Billingham, Eston and Redcar. Not, you will note, Hartlepool. So for a little

Figure 1. A map, the darker shaded area showing the area of Teesside? *Reproduced Courtesy of BT*

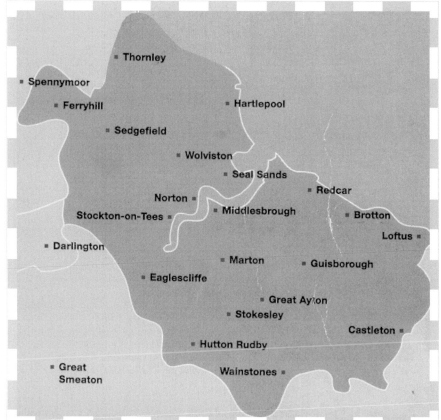

Figure 2. Signs abound throughout Northern England saying Teesside. In the middle of Hartlepool is a classic example. This quasi Mexican-style obelisk is labeled Teesside, but directly in front of it is a road sign giving directions to the south. A little further on is another sign telling the motorist that it is twelve miles to Teesside. *Author's collection*

while at least, people knew where Teesside was. But then came Cleveland County and confusion ruled again.

Today's official local authority boundaries are of little help in showing where Teesside is. The existing defined areas of the Police, Ambulance and Fire Service give us no help either so I would like you to consider the map (Figure 1). It refers to the area shown as 'Cleveland' and uses this area to define postcodes TS. Presumably the TS stands for Teesside. I think we can soon agree that this map is not a map of Teesside.

I am fascinated by this Teesside concept and would like to try and define what or where is Teesside. To accomplish this task we will have to go on a curious journey. I think most readers will agree that to be in Teesside a TS postcode is a prerequisite, but not everywhere with a TS code is of necessity in Teesside. Readers will I hope agree that Thornley, Ferryhill, Castleton and Sedgfield are not in Teesside, also that Darlington with a DL postcode is not part of it either (Figure 2).

Teesside is clearly not Cleveland, but if we had a City of Teesside where would it be, is it a place or a myth? I have asked many local residents in researching this article, the simple question 'How do we find Teesside?' If those who live in the area can't define it, how can

Figure 3. The bleak rail halt ringed by double yellow lines where the sign for Teesside Railway Station seems to be pointing to Alice's rabbit hole. *Author's collection*

visitors? Like all great explorers maybe we should set out to visit the place, find it for ourselves, go on a curious journey.

Any explorer in the twenty-first century would choose to use air travel as their means of transport, and it is easy to buy a ticket to Teesside International Airport from anywhere in the world. It will take you from most of the world's airports direct to Teesside.

At these airports simply follow the signs, board a plane and in a very short space of time the plane will land at Teesside, our very own airport. If you get the opportunity look out of the plane as it descends and see the river Tees and a mixture of sea, sand, industry, housing and some beautiful hills. Is this Teesside?

Through the airport just grab a cab and ask the driver to take you to Teesside. So he didn't, never mind, it's just a short walk to Teesside's very own railway station, that should solve our problem. It is called Teesside Airport Railway Station. Gateway to our new 'City Of Teesside?' It is an extraordinary station. No car park is available, it is ringed by double yellow lines and Oh Dear, the train only runs twice a week - two trains, both on a Saturday. No railway timetable I have ever read lists any destination as Teesside other than this bleak little rail halt (Figure 3).

Still in our hunt for TS we must press on. Leaving the little halt on foot we turn right, along the busy A67 and after a few minutes we reach a boundary sign for Stockton-on-Tees. No, that's not saying Teesside. Let us retrace our steps. Walking past the station we soon come to another big boundary sign. Yes we have reached Darlington. So Teesside's very own airport and our very special rail halt is located between those two towns. Is this Teesside then? Well no not really. As we walk back towards the station we might just see a hand written sign pointing to Lower Goosepool. Could that help us find Teesside? Well in an odd way it might, but before considering this, let's look at a few other things.

If we had tried to travel by main line train - same result. No trains with a destination called Teesside are listed. By road it is stranger still. Most main roads signs show Teesside – fifty miles, but as you approach the area they disappear and only county boundary signs tell us we are approaching Middlesbrough, Stockton, Hartlepool – most curious. Clearly we are not going to find Teesside by becoming modern day explorers, so let us try a different means. Let's consider Lower Goosepool as a route to finding Teesside.

As we look down at the steel rails at Teesside airport's railway halt, waiting in vain for a train to Teesside, let us try to become time travellers. Let's travel back in time some 176 years to 27 September

Figure 4. St Peter's Church, Croft. 'Tickets please' said the guard. 'I'm afraid I haven't got one' said Alice in a frightened tone, 'there wasn't a ticket office where I came from.' Lewis Carroll, *Alice Through the Looking Glass*. 1872. *Author's collection*

1825. That day we could have caught a train to Teesside all right. For it was here at Goosepool that *Locomotion No.1* on its inaugural journey stopped for water to fill its boiler. Was 27 September 1825 a Saturday I wonder! Not far from Goosepool is Croft, (Figure 4) here in the nineteenth century lived Lewis Carroll, 'father' of Alice

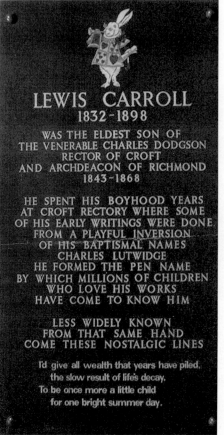

LEWIS CARROLL
1832-1898

WAS THE ELDEST SON OF
THE VENERABLE CHARLES DODGSON
RECTOR OF CROFT
AND ARCHDEACON OF RICHMOND
1843-1868

HE SPENT HIS BOYHOOD YEARS
AT CROFT RECTORY WHERE SOME
OF HIS EARLY WRITINGS WERE DONE
FROM A PLAYFUL INVERSION
OF HIS BAPTISMAL NAMES
CHARLES LUTWIDGE
HE FORMED THE PEN NAME
BY WHICH MILLIONS OF CHILDREN
WHO LOVE HIS WORKS
HAVE COME TO KNOW HIM

LESS WIDELY KNOWN
FROM THAT SAME HAND
COME THESE NOSTALGIC LINES

I'd give all wealth that years have piled,
the slow result of life's decay,
To be once more a little child
for one bright summer day.

Figure 5. The plaque for Alice's 'father' in St Peter's Church, Croft. *Author's collection*

(Figure 5). It was at Croft where the idea was formed for those immortal lines 'Curiouser and Curiouser said Alice'. Now, our Alice was a traveller who found many interesting places on her journeys. Maybe she can help us find Teesside. As Alice would have said about *Locomotion No.1s* destination – 'Teesside was not there before it started its journey and it only happened because it got there'. Yes, I believe Alice may have found Teesside. You see, it's not a place at all, more a sort of locality. Put simply, the rails of the Stockton & Darlington Train Company were to become the sinews of a new mighty industrial giant. A giant whose heart was most certainly steam powered. Everywhere that those rails stretched was soon to be transformed from marshes and farmland into a huge industrial conurbation.

Yes, Teesside is the area that was transformed by the world's first passenger railway. I think we may have finally defined Teesside.

When, on the morning of 27 September 1825, that little train travelled from Brussellton Bank to Stockton-on-Tees it had no headboard reading 'Teesside', but every little puff of that tiny engine took it towards its destination and by its travelling those twenty and a half miles, pulling just 80 tons, it made Teesside happen. How did all this come about?

After the Battle of Trafalgar in 1805 Britain was undisputedly master of the seas. The British Fleet controlled the trade routes across the world's oceans and of course ships were built of wood and powered by sail. The Industrial Revolution of the eighteenth century had been founded on water transport. The Grand Union Canal linked Birmingham to London. The Kennet & Avon provided London with access to a West Coast seaport at Bristol, so it was hardly surprising that in 1767 James Brindley was instructed to work out a route for a canal to link the Durham coalfields with the mouth of the Tees.

The route Brindley suggested was a thirty-three mile canal from Winston to Stockton-on-Tees. This canal – sixteen feet wide and five feet four inches deep - was budgeted at £63,722 (£3.5M in current terms). Whilst it may have seemed to offer advantages – one horse being able to do the work of thirty on land – there were a few drawbacks to consider. Clearly the Durham coalmines were in hilly terrain, not ideal canal territory. The Tees from Stockton was very shallow and extremely winding. In the near future would a canal have been able to transport the iron ore from the Cleveland Hills to Teesside blast furnaces?

The establishment of the Tees Navigation Company by Act of Parliament in 1808, and the opening of the Mandale Cut in 1810, both served to keep the canalites hopes alive. The cost of the canal venture kept escalating however and when in 1818 a public meeting was called in Stockton the cost had reached £205,283 (£6.5M today).

The meeting on 31 July 1818 in Stockton agreed to ask Parliament for the power to build a canal linking the river Gauntless at Evenwood with the Tees at Stockton and the meeting formed a company, Proprietors of the Stockton and Auckland Canal. They then tried to raise the £206,000. The noted Stockton solicitor, Raisbeck, was the only dissenter at the meeting from the Stockton contingent, whilst the Darlington representatives of Edward Pease and Jonathan Backhouse were aghast at the proposals of the canalites and resolved to fight the plans which meant Darlington being bypassed altogether. Joining together with Raisbeck, and the merchants of Yarm, they put into place plans for a railway to be built instead of a canal.

Looking back from the twenty first century it is not always clear how visionary were the pioneers who conceived the S&D Railway. Whilst tramways had existed, for many historians seem to agree the first wagon way, wooden rails and wooden wheels were conceived around 1615. Causey Arch Railway Bridge near Tanfield, built in 1727 demonstrates the longevity of the horse drawn coal wagons, but the whole concept of a steam-powered train was quite revolutionary. This is why the S&D Railway was planned as a horse drawn wagon way. Then on 19 April 1821 George Stephenson took a journey by stagecoach from Newcastle to Stockton-on-Tees. Stephenson then walked from Stockton to Darlington following the intended route of the railway. George Stephenson then visited Edward Pease at his home in Darlington and convinced him that he should use steam-powered locomotives to haul his trains. Much has been written on how Pease and his associates built the world's first passenger railway, so I will confine myself to the basics. For those wishing to learn more an excellent source is *The Stockton-Darlington Railway* by Norman Moorsom. This treasure trove of information about the events of the 1820-30s is quite incredible reading. A most excellent website also exists at www.Stocktondarlingtonrailway.co.uk with information for those wanting to visit the area of the line.

When Pease, Backhouse and Raisbeck left the meeting held by the canalites in 1818 they were determined to build a railway and so they did. Public meetings were called, but not without setbacks in great numbers and on 5 April 1819 Parliament threw out the first Bill to *Establish a Railway* by 106 votes to 93.

Not discouraged Pease fought on. He was faced with a very difficult situation. The Stockton folk wanted to build a canal, the local Durham landowners did not want a railway at any price on their land and Pease needed to raise the capital.

When, on 29 January 1820, King George III died, it meant a new King and new Parliament, so it was to be 1821 before another meeting could sit to re-consider the railway bills. After the King's death the pioneers met at the *George and Dragon* in Yarm. They employed George Overton to make a new survey. In 1821 a new bill was started – first reading 20 February, second reading 28 February, then the committee stage. When Pease's team read the small print, they found eighty per cent of the money had to be raised. In desperation Pease put up £7,000 of his own capital (about £250,000 today). The project was saved, and the committee stage was passed. Third reading 12 April, House of Lords 17 April and on 19 April the Bill received the Royal Assent from George IV. By a strange coincidence this was the very same day Pease and Stephenson met at Pease's Darlington home.

Anyone could run a wagon on it providing they paid the going rate, used safe equipment between the hours of 7.00 am and 6.00 pm in winter and 5.00 am and 10.00 pm in summer – and they shut the gates behind them. Despite all this minutiae, it is what is missing that most interests us.

There is no mention of coal exporting – yet within a few years the Port of Middlesbrough would be founded as the export trade blossomed. There is no mention of steam engines just that the wagons would be hauled by 'men or horses or otherwise' – yet within years *Locomotion No. 1* and its successors had proved the durability of the new-fangled technology. And there is no mention of 'passengers' – yet the S&DRs greatest claim to fame is that it was the world's first passenger railway. So, while the good folk of Stockton wanted a canal and the politicians expected a little tramway, Pease and Stephenson got together and built a steam railway. Many battles had been fought over these schemes before the horse lost out to the steam and rails superseded canals. The result however is clear. Put all these things together and what happened next was Teesside.

Thus I believe we have identified the creative force that made Teesside happen. But who founded it and where is it today, we will need some more time travel at this stage to help us find out.

Let us move forward to 27 December 1830 and join a small train as it leaves Darlington, what was special about this train? This train was going to Port Darlington about four miles further down the new branch line from Stockton. On our arrival gun salutes and great crowds with banners would meet us. Why such a welcome? Well on that train were the founders of S&DR and they are making the inaugural journey to Middlesbrough. It may be December but let us also join the 600 guests who are enjoying a cold collation from a table of 134 yards in length. But once the crowds go home and the train departs what is left at this bleak spot on the Tees.

The Census of 1831 records:

<u>Middlesbrough Township</u>
Houses: 26 occupied by 30 families; none uninhabited
Persons: 89 males: 69 females: total 154
Occupations: 15 families chiefly employed in agriculture
              5 families chiefly employed in trade,
              manufacturing and handicraft
              10 other families not comprised in the two
              preceding classes.

Yet today if Teesside has a capital then it has to be Middlesbrough, once known as Port Darlington and described by Prime Minister Gladstone as 'This Infant Hercules' it is now the by far largest town in the Tees area. But in those days all its mail was sent c/o Stockton-on-Tees Post Office. Some infant, some Hercules!

The Stockton to Darlington Railway Bill dated 1828 had extended those steel sinews from Stockton to deeper water on the banks of the Tees at Middlesbrough. Within a few years vast quantities of coal were being exported to London and overseas. Soon, however, Port Clarence was to become the coal export centre on the Tees.

At Middlesbrough, Cleveland iron ore was combined with Durham coal to make 'Ironopolis' and thus Middlesbrough became a booming iron and steel town.

Figure 6. A mural of Locomotion No.1 that is displayed in Darlington's North Road Museum and was made by pupils from Skerne Primary School in Darlington. *Author's collection*

But let us travel forward now twenty years. We find the area has been transformed. Henry Bolckow is speaking at the time of the discovery of Eston Iron Ore. This man who founded Middlesbrough, is also attributed to being the Founder of Teesside. In his book of the same name Ron Gott quotes Bolckow as saying in 1850:

> It would not, we believe, however, require any great stretch of imagination to anticipate the time when Middlesbrough, having as the center of a great iron trade, eclipsed Birmingham, shall have increased to such an extent with Redcar and its noble harbour completed, as one suburb, and Stockton the other.

So in 1850 we have heard the concept of Teesside defined, but after this fine speech we should travel forward in time to see if Bolckow's vision of the future was accurate. After any great triumph the Romans would build a triumphal arch. So it was that seventy-four years after the coming of the S&D railway the worthy citizens of Middlesbrough followed their example. On 17 October 1911, Prince Arthur of Connaught declared the regions best-known landmark open. It's called 'The Transporter' (Figure 6) and its huge structure towers over the Teesside landscape to this day. It is a giant triumphal steel arch for a town built on roots of steel. If Teesside has a capital then 'Teesside City' would be Middlesbrough and its population of 144,000 (mid 2000) makes it the second largest town. It houses the area's Law Courts and much else besides. But Bolckow was incorrect in predicting that Middlesbrough would be the biggest town in Teesside. Stockton-on-Tees, birthplace of the safety match, is the area's largest town, with a population of 178,300 (mid-2000). Readers may care to ponder the whys and wherefores, but that's how it is.

Now, however, we must end our time travelling and simply travel along the existing railway from Darlington to Saltburn. Most of the area we pass through is, I believe in Teesside. I believe most would agree that Stockton, Thornaby, Eaglescliffe and Yarm are certainly part of Teesside. The S&DR railway certainly went there, but what about Redcar and Saltburn?

When you take the train to Saltburn, you will find a most pleasant town, the S&DR got to Saltburn in 1861. As you leave the station look about you at all the buildings. Many are a whitish hue. The colour is from bricks made on Durham coalfields from pit spoil and the town exists because the railway made it happen. So if we accept that those mighty steel tentacles reached here from Darlington, maybe this and nearby Redcar reached by S&DR in 1846 are also part of Teesside.

The north bank of the river is a more complex matter as in many ways; S&DR was not the main rail company in this area. Here the Clarence Rail Company was supreme and when in 1852 the Hartlepool Railway took over the Clarence, great local rivalries continued a pace. In spite of this fact Port Clarence, Billingham, and Haverton Hill are generally looked on as being in Teesside, but what about Hartlepool?

Not too many years ago I attended a dinner where a well-known Teesside politician gave a speech on our membership of the EU. The loudest laughter of the evening from his predominately Middlesbrough audience was when he said 'I don't know how we get the people of Hartlepool into Europe, they won't even join Cleveland.' Well, as I was born a Hartlepudlian, and have worked there for forty-four years I know why they didn't care for Cleveland. Any readers who wish to know about these affairs should talk to politicians of all shades of opinion. In fact I can think of no other topic which has ever united Hartlepool folk more than their total opposition to Cleveland County. Inviting me, a Hartlepool man to write about Teesside is a bit like asking a turkey to write about

Christmas. Historically, Hartlepool was always a Durham town. The Tees was a barrier, not an artery. Yorkshire ended at the south bank of the Tees. Born on that southern bank and you could play cricket for the white rose county. The County Palatine 'Land of the Prince Bishops' began at the northern banks of the Tees. In olden days sanctuary was to be had by grasping the great doorknocker of Durham Cathedral. Part of Teesside indeed!

In that great reference guide *Highlights in the History of Cleveland* compiled by Norman Moorsom, readers will find the very first town mentioned is Hartlepool and in that book's first few pages it is the town mentioned most. As this book points out, Cleveland took its name from the region that lay between the rivers Tees and Esk, so what this Cleveland area thing has to do with Hartlepool has long been a mystery to many in our town. Is Hartlepool part of Teesside? That though is a bit more difficult question.

Hartlepool starting to become a coal exporting port was clearly thanks to the building of the Stockton and Darlington railway, albeit S&DR never itself ran directly to the town of Hartlepool. Its first coal shipment began in 1833 thanks to coal transported from the north via the Haswell and Wellfield rail link. Then the second link in a southerly direction to the Clarence Railway was built and finally a coastal rail link northwards to Sunderland.

So if my definition of Teesside is that it is an area whose economy was transformed by the S&DR, maybe Hartlepool does not qualify. Do not let us be pedantic here however because the railways in our area were really all the 'sons and daughters' of the S&DR Company. All too soon all were to become part one of the worlds first great monopolies, NER (North Eastern Railway Company).

Shortly before this however the Hartlepool Railway took over the Clarence Railway and the town of West Hartlepool was born. From that date till the present day most people in this neck of the woods have been too busy feuding between 'Crofters' and 'West Dockers' to worry about Teesside.

With the developments at Seal Sands, the building of the Nuclear Power Station on the north bank of the Tees, and general extension of the town's boundaries, Hartlepool is certainly now on the banks of the Tees and some areas of it may be said to be on the side of the Tees.

I am often reminded of the paradox of Wells-next-to-the-Sea. When you get to this Norfolk town you find that the sea has gone away, and Wells is not next the sea at all.

Hartlepool is now, however, more than ever next to the Tees and economically it is part of Teesside, albeit historically, it was always part of County Durham.

If the sea has moved away from Wells, the Tees has certainly moved nearer to Hartlepool. Not, you will note, that Hartlepool has moved nearer to the Tees.

The railways made Hartlepool, as they did Middlesbrough, but with its long traditions and its ancient charter from 1201, I feel that its people have always guarded their heritage and independence. Time will, I believe, eventually prove that it's not only by its TS postcode that Hartlepool is now in reality part of Teesside.

In my youth we had our own steel works the 'South Durham' and its worthy of mention that the two serious attempts to merge this company with Middlesbrough's Dorman Long were both scuppered by Hartlepool industrialists and other local worthies.

What a contrast it is in today's situation with Corus and the global economy, when two local steel giants could not even come together as a single entity.

So a town, which is steeped in a long history as part of Durham, really needs to find its place in the twenty first century maybe just maybe its time to agree we are going to have to be part of Teesside.

Readers wishing to further explore these facts are warned however, please exercise extreme caution if you venture onto the headland of Hartlepool. Passing through the ghostly shadows of the now demolished Throston Bridge, in sight of the magnificent vista of St Hilda's Church, here you will meet great characters who will deny both hanging monkeys and having anything at all to do with 'West' let alone Teesside. You have been warned!

Conclusion

The areas around the two other great North East rivers Tyne & Wear were well established at the start of the nineteenth century. Teesside did not really exist as such, but its major assets were all in place. Ample coal deposits existed to the north and the west, huge iron ore resources in the Cleveland Hills, a mighty river that could be made navigable, and vast salt deposits. What was needed to turn this sleeping giant into a major industrial conurbation?

Pease and Backhouse saw all too clearly the huge potential when founding Middlesbrough and Hartlepool folk were also clearly involved in the affairs of Teesside at this time.

A newspaper report of 12 February 1831 records that after the opening of a new 'cut' on the 10 February in the Tees at Stockton, a grand dinner was held at the Town House, Stockton. Among the

Figure 7. The Transporter Bridge, a magnificent feat of Victorian engineering. *Author's collection*

noted guests were W Ward Jackson and Hartlepool's noted historian Sir Cuthbert Sharp (Figure 7). Also worthy of note, in the chair at that dinner was ML Raisbeck, the great railway campaigner.

It is my contention that the S&DR provided the spark needed to trigger the development around the river Tees and so caused Teesside to happen. Without these farsighted railway pioneers it perhaps could have been oh so different. As a tribute to their fortitude and perseverance I would like to end with this cutting from the *Durham Chronicle,* 1 January 1831:

> *We cannot conclude this account, without offering to the Railway Company our most cordial congratulations upon the manner in which they have carried to a successful termination the great design in the*

Figure 8. The noted historian, Sir Cuthbert Sharp's house in Old Hartlepool before demolition in the 1950s. *Author's collection*

prosecution of which they have been so long engaged, and in which they have persevered, through good and evil report, with a firmness and energy of which there are but few examples. Much might be said of the difficulties they have had to encounter, but only to combat to overcome. Into such a dissertation, however, it is not our intention at present to enter; and we shall content ourselves with observing that they have triumphed alike over the face of nature, private cupidity, and magisterial hostility. This they have done; and the least return that, or the public, for whose sake they have adventured so much, can wish them is, that where they have sown they may reap, and that a hundred fold.

Without them Tees Port would not now be one of the largest ports in Britain, handling millions of tonnes per annum. So, yes with some help from Alice, a steam train named *Locomotion No. 1*, and our imagination, I believe we have found Teesside.

Author's note
It is perhaps worth a mention that the author's father, Alderman TH Pailor, bought the house that once occupied a site next to St Hilda's Church that was the birthplace of the noted historian Cuthbert Sharp. The council placed a compulsory purchase order on the property and it was demolished. When a hue and cry ensued because of the historical significance of the property, the council apologised saying that they had knocked down the wrong house. As there were no adjoining buildings left by the time that particular house was demolished, one wonders how a mistake such as that could have been made!

2. A Big Day Out at Port Darlington: and How Ainsley Managed to Miss It

by Norman Moorsom

THE WHOLE SPECTRUM OF HISTORY both prehistoric and recorded has been divided for convenience into periods, each of which has a clear title to distinguish it from all others. What is not always clear, however, is whether a particular period has a specifically dated beginning and end. Against this background of broad periods with rather vaguely defined edges, it is very satisfying to be able to present to the reader a study which can be narrowed down to a small number of precisely dated events.

The Teesside area underwent extensive and fundamental, indeed life changing change during that period of history which we call the Industrial Revolution, particularly in its later stages during the first half of the nineteenth century. In this context, it is possible to highlight a number of specific dates, exact points in time, which, in themselves, may be regarded as crucial milestones in the economic and social history of the region.

One of these dates is associated with the particular events which lie at the heart of this chapter, but I feel that it is important at the outset to place it firmly into a more general context. As we will see, it is a date, which not only marks a significant development in the general evolution of a regional industry but also represents the extension of that industry as a local factor in relation to the actual birth of a community. It is also a date, which must have been indelibly engraved upon the memory of one individual, for whom the events of a very promising day suddenly went terribly wrong.

Exactly forty years later, a group of gentlemen met together in order to celebrate the anniversary of that day and we are in the privileged position of being able to eavesdrop on their reminiscences. Such a situation emphasizes the value of oral sources to the local historian, in terms of eyewitness realism. In this particular case, it also demonstrates the fact that nostalgia is not a modern phenomenon. I am hoping that you have already been asking yourself what industry it might be which was of such significance to those who were involved in its commemoration and I suspect that, if you are thinking in terms of outstanding Victorian developments in our area, you may well have deduced that we will be looking at the iron and steel trade. This, however, is not the case. We are, in fact, concerned with the transporting and exporting of County Durham coal.

The miners of Northern England have had a proud tradition of wresting black gold from the bowels of the earth and the closure of pit after pit in more recent times has been the cause of great economic change and great heartache. By the dawn of the nineteenth century, the rivers Tyne and Wear were already well established as centres for the export of coal and from the year 1810 plans began to take shape which ultimately led to the establishing of a rival Tees-based trade. Initially, however, the main objective of the group of businessmen involved in the scheme was to consider the best possible means of transporting not only coal, but also lead and lime from outlying areas of County Durham to Stockton.

For several years, the matter was debated in terms of a choice between establishing a canal or a railway. The former option was favoured by the Stockton element within the group, while support for the latter came from Darlington. The main driving force behind the railway scheme was Edward Pease of Darlington (Figure 1) the owner of a woollen mill in that town, and it was this scheme that was finally adopted. The first prospectus of the Stockton and Darlington Railway Company was issued in the following year. The final version of the amended Bill actually received the Royal Assent in 1824. In the meantime, the first rail had been laid on 23 May 1822, but it was not until 27 September 1825 that the formal opening of the main line took place. It was, indeed, a day of great rejoicing, on which the engine *Locomotion No.1* drew a number of passenger coaches in addition to the coal wagons. This specific date in 1825 heralded the dawn of a new era in the region's own Industrial Revolution – a ground-breaking development from which there was to be no going back. At the same time, the wider significance of the event must not be overlooked, for the Stockton & Darlington was the first steam-powered passenger railway in the world. In strictly economic terms, the company's directors had a dual aim: to transport coal for sale in inland areas and to export it from Stockton to a number of ports in the South of England.

Figure 1. Edward Pease of Darlington, known as the Father of the Railways, he was the head of the Quaker dynasty to which our northern region owes so much. *Author's collection*

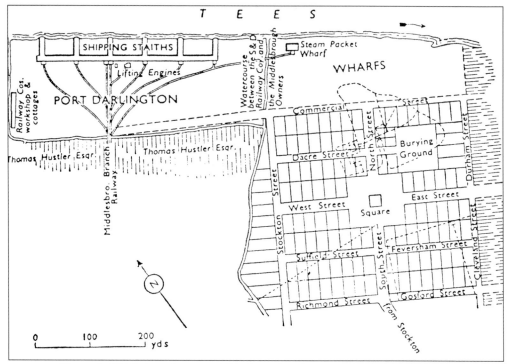

Figure 2. Middlesbrough was established as a dormitory town for those involved in the work at Port Darlington. The highlighted watercourse was actually the boundary between the parishes of Acklam to the west and Middlesbrough to the east. *Author's collection*

The first coal was shipped from the Tees on 26 January 1826, thus inaugurating a Tees-based export trade, and it soon became clear that the bustling trade was becoming a victim of its own success. Access to the Stockton Staiths from the North Sea was hampered by distance, the tortuous nature of the river channel, navigational hazards of shoals, sandbanks and an occasional island, and the shallowness of the river itself at the staiths, which had a limiting effect on the size of vessels that could be accommodated there. The directors must have been well satisfied with the initial success of their venture, but acknowledged that there was no scope for the long-term expansion, which its potential indicated.

The geographical and natural phenomena which conspired against the further development of a Stockton-based export trade were to pave the way for the setting-up of alternative shipping facilities at a specially-chosen site across the river in the North Riding of Yorkshire, to be known as Port Darlington, (Figure 2) and, as a direct result, the founding of the dormitory town of Middlesbrough, which took its name from the farm on the site. The creation of the Middlesbrough Branch Railway, running from Stockton to a place of naturally deeper water, and the planning and building of the nearby

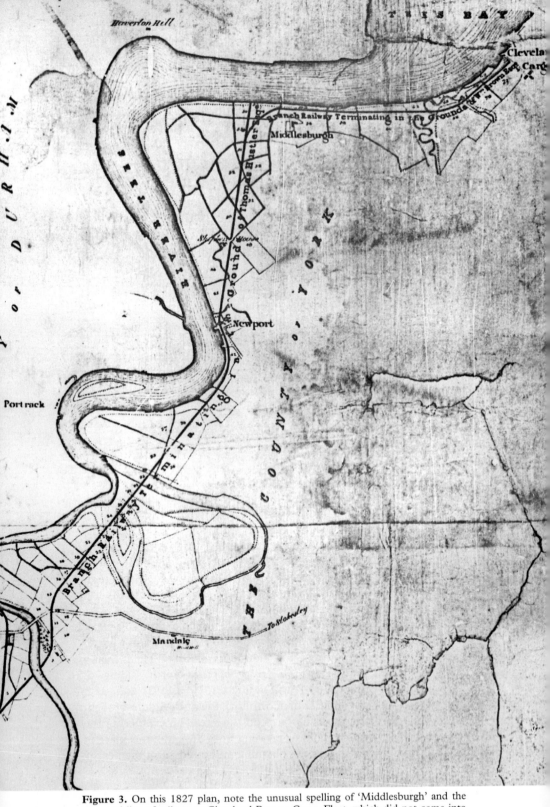

Figure 3. On this 1827 plan, note the unusual spelling of 'Middlesburgh' and the proposed line of railway to Cleveland Port or Cargo Fleet, which did not come into being until the Redcar branch was constructed in the 1840s. *Author's collection*

Figure 4. The Tees Suspension Bridge was designed by Captain Samuel Brown RN. This elegant structure proved too weak to bear the weight of large numbers of coal wagons and was replaced by an iron bridge in 1842. *Author's collection*

town were, in fact, separate business ventures in terms of their financial promotion, but they did evolve concurrently and the combined projects were highlighted for the public on 27 December 1830 (Figure 3).

By that point in time, the river Tees had been crossed by an elegant railway suspension bridge, which was the first structure of its kind in the world, the branch railway was completed to Port Darlington and house-building in Middlesbrough had been under way for some eight months (Figure 4).

An advertisement was placed in local newspapers as an invitation to the public to witness the inauguration of the Middlesbrough Branch Railway, also involving the suspension bridge and the coal staiths (Figure 5). The stage was well and truly set for a red-letter day in relation to the industrial and economic evolution of the region. It was, indeed, a clear case history in the making and large numbers of locals turned out in order to see it all unfold. There must have been a keen awareness of the unique significance of these developments in rural north Cleveland, the Middlesbrough Branch being the first rail to enter the region and Middlesbrough itself being the first town to

Figure 5. The announcement of the opening of the Middlesbrough Branch Railway in the *Durham County Advertiser* on 24 December 1830. Note the additional 'o' in Middlesbrough. *Author's collection*

THE Public are informed, that the OPENING of the MIDDLESBOROUGH BRANCH RAILWAY (being an extension of the Stockton and Darlington Railway to deep water in the River Tees), will take place on MONDAY NEXT, the 27th inst.

By order, R. OTLEY.

Railway Office, Darlington, Dec. 20, 1830.

Figure 6. Designed by Timothy Hackworth of New Shildon, the six staiths were revolutionary, in that the mechanical lowering of the blocks of coal into the ship's hold preserved their size and consequently, their market value. *Author's collection*

be established as a direct result of the process of railway expansion (Figure 6). For all those who decided to witness the events for themselves, it certainly promised to be a big day out.

A labourer named Ainsley, a resident of Newton Bewley, near Billingham may well have read about the event in the *Durham County Advertiser* on Christmas Eve, or he may simply have heard about it on the grapevine. He made up his mind to cross the river into Yorkshire, possibly by means of the ancient ford at Newport, and to make his way east to Port Darlington. As he walked along the riverside path near Newport, he might have spotted the public house close to the railway, of which Mr Marshall was the landlord, and where he may well have fancied having a jar of ale and a warm-through on the way home. Ainsley found himself walking alongside the procession of coaches and coal wagons which had begun its journey at Stockton and was approaching the staiths at Port Darlington. He decided that he would complete the journey by hitching a lift on one of the coaches, but in trying to scramble aboard he slipped and fell. As a result, one of the wheels passed over his leg and fractured it. This incident and the events which followed it were not mentioned at all in the subsequent newspaper report and the only source of information relating to them is a document associated with a dispute which arose over liability for the payment of the expenses which were incurred in Ainsley's medical treatment. The Public Record Office holds this document and it came to light during a general search for material relating to the Port Darlington shipping staiths. It reveals the fact that the main objective of those who became involved in the drama which followed Ainsley's accident was clearly the prompt removal of the victim from the scene:

He was immediately, & without any notice to the parish officers placed by the persons present in a coach attached to a Steam engine & conveyed back along the railway, about a mile, to Newport, a hamlet through which it passes, in Linthorp township, where the coach stopped at a small public house, close to the railway, kept by one Marshall in which there are only three lodging rooms at that time all occupied.

Marshall was informed by one of the attendants that a man had got his leg broke & that they must leave him there till a Surgeon could be procured. –Marshall at first refused to receive him, alleging the want of room in his house, & said he had better be taken somewhere else. –A Stranger proposed that he should be taken to Stockton, which is the nearest town where a surgeon could be had, & about three miles from Newport. –On the attendants repeating that they must leave him at Marshall's, the caller said he must first see Mr Simpson one of the Linthorp Overseers & who lived next door. –Finding, on enquiry, that Mr Simpson was absent, & the attendants insisting that Ainsley should be left, Marshall consented to receive him, & a form upon which to convey him, was brought out of the house, & placed alongside the coach. When on the point of being taken out Another Stranger spoke to the attendants, & said that, as the steam was up, they should, by all means, take him to Stockton, as he might be removed thither before a messenger could arrive there for a surgeon. The coach door was again shut, & the engine immediately proceeded with the coach towards Stockton. The coach stopped where the high road leading towards Stockton crosses the railway & Ainsley was removed to a public house a few yards on the Stockton road kept by Mark Ryder which is in the township of Thornaby in the county of York, & about 1/4 of a mile from Stockton which is on the opposite side of the Tees. –Mr Milburn, a surgeon from Stockton, was called in; by whom, it is not known. It being more convenient for Mr Milburn to give the requisite attendance at Stockton he engaged a lodging there to which Ainsley was removed the next day, and there attended him until he recovered.

Mr Milburn however states that his motive for removing Ainsley to Stockton was Ryder's positive refusal to permit him to remain longer in his house. –Mr Milburn, soon after his attendance commenced, made an application to Mr Pease one of the railway Compy, who, it is understood tho' not ascertained promised that he or the Compy would pay the expenses that might be incurred in consequence of the accident.

Mr Pearson & Mr Simpson, The Overseers of the Poor of Linthorp, were at the staiths where the accident happened & were informed of it a few minutes afterwards, but not until after Ainsley had been removed from thence. They were applied to by Mr Milburn on the 29 Decr to pay the expense incurred at Ryder's, but they declined to interfere at all in the business conceiving that Linthorp was not liable.

The Railway Company have paid part of Mr Milburn's bill and he claims the remainder of the Overseers of Linthorp.

The expense of Ainsley's board & lodging at Stockton has been paid by the parish officers of that place, who claim to be reimbursed by the Overseers of Linthorp.

The probability of the occurrence of similar accidents renders the question in this case of considerable importance to the townsp of Linthorp.

Within the context of claims for reimbursement by the surgeon and the Overseers of the Poor of Stockton, Ainsley was clearly involved, albeit as a pawn rather than a player, in a test case, from the point of view of the Overseers of the Poor of Linthorpe, who suspected, and quite reasonably so, that his accident may not be an isolated incident in relation to the expanding railway system. He was, indeed, not the first to suffer an accident on the occasion of a formal railway opening ceremony, for on 15 September 1830 the Rt Hon William Huskisson, MP for Liverpool, had actually been killed in an incident at the inauguration of the Liverpool & Manchester Railway. Even if Ainsley had actually been aware of his comparative good fortune, it may well have been of little comfort to him as he was, quite literally being shunted around between Port Darlington, Newport, Thornaby and Stockton. In addition to suffering the pain of the injury, which must have been considerable, there was also the humiliation of knowing that he was both an embarrassment and an inconvenience to all involved in attempting to sort out what appeared to be a rather complicated situation. This sort of historical incident certainly bears interesting comparison with problems experienced by individuals requiring care within the modern National Health Service.

For exactly a month after the accident, until 27 January 1831, Mr Milburn's expenses had been covered by the Railway Company, but they felt that thereafter they were no longer obliged to be involved. The surgeon had clearly met resistance from Mark Ryder in terms of Ainsley staying longer in his house at Thornaby and it was at the suggestion of Mr Pease, a director of the Railway Company, that he was moved to a more convenient situation. It is not clear as to

Figure 7. Many of those who attended the opening of the Middlesbrough Branch Railway proudly wore this medal suspended from a ribbon. *Author's collection*

whether this was Joseph Pease, a prime mover in promoting the Middlesbrough Branch Railway and the creation of the new Town of Middlesbrough, or his younger brother Henry, who was also present on that auspicious occasion. Mr Milburn's medical attendance had continued until 8 April, at the expense of the Overseers of Stockton, who claimed that their counterparts in Linthorpe should reimburse them.

The complex matter was not settled until 3 January 1832, and that was not by the mutual consent of the parties involved. Far from it, in fact, for the case had been referred to a lawyer based in Chancery Lane in London for his opinion as arbitrator. The signature to his legal statement appears to be J Chitty and he ruled in favour of the Linthorpe Overseers, stating that they were not liable for any of the expenses involved in Ainsley's medical care.

There is no indication that this care lasted until he was fully fit again, but it can be imagined that every step which he took for months after the accident would have been a painful reminder of that anticipated big day out that went so badly wrong. It is to be hoped that Ainsley would also have managed to acquire a less personal souvenir of the day, in the shape of one of the handsome medals, which were made available as keepsakes of the events of 27 December 1830. One side depicts the shipping staiths at Port Darlington and the other the railway suspension bridge on the river Tees between Stockton and Thornaby (Figure 7).

If Ainsley had access to the *Durham Chronicle* of 1 January 1831,

Figure 8. A close up view of one of the Port Darlington coal staiths. *Author's collection*

he would have been able to read the report of the exciting events that he had missed, something of which he may well have heard in the background as he was being bundled between Port Darlington and Newport. After placing the Middlesbrough Branch Railway project into the context of the evolution of the S&D Railway itself, the account described the progress of the flag-bedecked rolling stock from Stockton. Time was allowed for the inspection of the suspension bridge across the Tees, then it was onwards for 'Middlesbro':

> *On arriving at Middlesbro', the procession was received with loud acclamation by the assembled multitude, and the firing of guns from vessels on the river and of others on shore. Flags of every size and description, from the Union Jack of England downward, floated on the breeze from the roofs of the respective buildings, and the day being uncommonly fine, the appearance of the whole was highly picturesque and beautiful.*
>
> *The Staiths are of great dimensions, (Figure 8) and are so*

constructed that six vessels can be loaded at the same time, while berths for the accommodation of others are formed between the drops. The banks of the river being low, the wagons are placed on a cradle on which they are hoisted by steam on to the Staith, from whence the coals are lowered into the ship with astonishing celerity. The river Tees at Middlesbro' is both broad and deep; and the increased facilities which the extension of the railway to this point will present, in the shipment not only of coal, but of every other commodity, compared with the difficulties and dangers of the navigation to Stockton, must be too palpable not to be appreciated by all who are concerned with the traffic of the port.

The process of shipping the Coals having been completed, a large body of the Railway Proprietors, their officers and friends, sat down to an excellent cold collation, which had been prepared with every attention to the convenience and comfort of the guests. A table 134 yards (123 metres) in length was set out in part of the principal gallery of the Staiths, which is covered in, and the whole was so arranged as to render the company insensible to the severity of the frost. Nearly 600 persons partook of the good cheer, and as the gallery was well lighted with portable gas, it may be readily conceived that the effect produced was equally agreeable and brilliant.

The whole tone of this newspaper article was of celebration in relation to the inaugural ceremonies of the day and congratulation in relation to those who were involved in the Middlesbrough Branch railway project. It is to be regretted that the account did not include even a brief listing of the more notable guests within the gathering of 600, but it is clear that the day's events had a lasting effect on a number of those involved.

On 27 December 1870, an anniversary celebration was held in Middlesbrough's original Town Hall, which still stands today in the centre of what used to be the market place. It was opened in 1846, a year which had also witnessed the final demolition of the solitary and legendary Middlesbrough farmhouse, on the lands of which the modern town had been established. Joseph Pease of Darlington and five partners had purchased the farm and its estates in 1829, all fellow Quakers, who adopted the title Owners of the Middlesbrough Estate.

The anniversary gathering itself was organised by William Fallows, (Figure 9) who forty years earlier had been the staiths master at Port Darlington with the responsibility of overseeing the shipping of the

first cargo of coal on board the *Sunniside*. He
had a great feeling for the past and may be
regarded   as   Middlesbrough's   first
historian. In studying his life and times in
some detail, I have come to the
conclusion that he was the instigator
of many schemes and events which
would simply not have materialised if
he had not taken the initiative.

Fallows himself presided at the
1870 gathering, during which there
were numerous long speeches and
just as many enthusiastic toasts. We
can now element to the events of
four decades earlier and complement
very nicely the newspaper report of
January 1831. It is, in fact, from
another newspaper that we are able to
glean the details of the later event. The
Middlesbrough News and Cleveland Advertiser
of 30 December 1870 stated:

*The CHAIRMAN then called upon the
company to fill up a bumper for the next
toast, which was one in which he had to
ask them to unite with him in
commemorating of that town forty years
ago. Referring to that period he said that
they then had no place in history and no
mark on the map of this country. At that time, in the one house that
stood within about 100 yards [92.3 metres] from where they were
then assembled, and another about half a mile away, there were only
about twenty five persons, but what there was now they all knew as
well as himself.*

*Well, what was it that brought them all there? It was the opening of
the Middlesbrough branch of the Stockton and Darlington Railway.
The powers to make that branch were attained only after a very great
struggle. Many of those who were interested in the coal trade were much
opposed to their obtaining powers to ship coals at Middlesbrough, and
opposed that measure at every stage of its progress. The committees of
the House of Commons in those days were very differently composed
from what they are now, and mostly consisted of gentlemen connected*

Figure 9. William Fallows, who was
known as the Father of Middlesbrough
and of the Tees, was associated with
the town for sixty years, from its
planning to his death in 1889. *Author's
collection*

with the districts in which such works were proposed to be carried out, and it required very great energy, perseverance and policy in obtaining such papers... However, the powers they sought were attained, and that day forty years ago was shipped from that port in the Sunniside the first cargo of coal. Since then Middlesbrough always appeared to be on the sunny side (Laughter).

During the course of these celebratory proceedings, there must have been a keen awareness of the absence of many who had been present at the original function, and at the end of his address (which had evolved into a local history lecture), William Fallows drew attention to the principal absentee with a toast to 'the health of Mr Joseph Pease, (Figure 10) the founder of the coal trade of South Durham and Middlesbrough'. It was he, indeed who had, to a great extent, provided the 'very great energy, perseverance and policy' in obtaining the Parliamentary Act which was necessary for the Middlesbrough scheme to proceed.

Figure 10. Joseph Pease was a railway pioneer and the founder of the town of Middlesbrough. He is depicted here in 1833, when he became the first Quaker Member of Parliament. *Author's collection*

Joseph Pease had actually withdrawn from public life several years earlier, when he finally lost his failing eyesight, and it was his younger brother Harry who responded to the toast on his behalf. In doing so, he shared with those present his memories of that distant day at Port Darlington, with a touch more realism than that demonstrated by the writer of the contemporary report in the *Durham Chronicle*:

The toast was drunk with great enthusiasm.
Mr HENRY PEASE (Figure 11) responded to the toast and in the course of his address said he thanked them most heartily for the kind manner in which they had received the toast of the health of his brother, Mr Joseph Pease. The worthy chairman had set them a very excellent example, and in the remarks he had made in reference to the

Figure 11. Henry Pease, a younger brother of Joseph, is noted as the founder of the Victorian resort of Saltburn-by-the-Sea. *Author's collection*

opening of the Middlesbrough Branch of the railway, he brought back to his mind the circumstances attending the opening.

The day on which it took place was one not entirely dissimilar to that on which they were then assembled. It was a cold wintry day and the place in which they met was a cold shed, very imperfectly warmed and lighted. Notwithstanding all that was done to make the place comfortable, it was but with little effect, and it was found necessary by some of the gentlemen to take on board an amount of champagne, which it was said, had more than the usual effect on them (Laughter).

It would be superfluous for him to refer to other changes that had taken place upon the banks of the river, but he ought not to admit to refer to that single house, to which allusion had already been made, which stood about 100 yards from the spot on which they were then assembled... Of that house he remembered, it was a great accommodation as the first place where the committee met to consider what was necessary for the promotion of the trading interests of the river. He believed the reason why they had met that day under such circumstances was because from the first they had pursued a liberal and honourable policy (Applause). Reference had been made to the first shipment of coals... and so they carried out the project with spirit, hoping for better days, and those better days had now dawned on them.

Several others followed the addresses of Messrs Fallows and Pease, the proceedings being interspersed by numerous toasts, and it is clear that a good time was had by one and all. It must have been very satisfying for those who had taken part in the events of 1830 to realise how far the town and its industries had developed within not much more than a generation. At the time of the third national census in 1831, Middlesbrough's population stood at 154 but by 1871 it had risen to 39,284. This remarkable statistic represents a percentage increase of 2,550 per cent. For those who had witnessed the entire evolution from green fields to heavy industry and street after street of terraced housing, it must have had something of a dream-like quality about it. There is certainly no doubting the fact that these early pioneers were men of clear vision and enterprise who had a steadfast faith in the future.

By 1870 the pioneers were in a position to acknowledge that that future had arrived and I personally find it quite fascinating to hear their story in their own words. For many years, I have found myself in the situation of reading yesterdays news with a view to writing today's history, and in studying the previous quoted report in the *Middlesbrough News* and *Cleveland Advertiser* of December 1870, I have imagined it being read on the day itself by a retired labourer in Newton Bewley. As he puts the paper aside, he rises, smiling ruefully to himself as he limps slowly across to the solid walnut dresser and removes a medal from the top drawer. It is an original Middlesbrough Branch Railway medal and its owner's name is Ainsley.

Sources and suggested reading

1. *Durham Chronicle*, January 1 1831.
2. Public Record Office, RAIL 667/479 CAPS 28115 1832.
3. *Middlesbrough News* and *Cleveland Advertiser*, December 30 1870.
4. Fordyce W, *A History of Coal, Coke and Coal Fields and the Manufacture of Iron in the North of England*, 1860.
5. Moorsom N, *The Birth and Growth of Modern Middlesbrough*, 1967. *The Stockton and Darlington Railway: The Foundation of Middlesbrough*, 1975. *A Journey through the History of Middlesbrough 1993.*
6. Jeans J S, *History of the Stockton and Darlington Railway 1875.*
7. McDougall C A, *The Stockton and Darlington Railway 1821-1863 1975.*
8. North G A, *Teesside's Economic Heritage 1975.*
9. Tomlinson W W, *The North Eastern Railway-Its Rise and Development 1914.*

3. WHAT'S IN A NAME?

by Simon Chapman

A REPORT IN A LOCAL NEWSPAPER some years ago described how a colliery village in the North East could look to the future by having the 'colliery' deleted from its name and replaced by 'by-the-sea' or some other such addition, simply to improve the perceived status of the place, in view of the demise of the afore-mentioned industrial site.

The impact on me of reading this piece of news was heightened by the discovery that it was a local historian that was so supportive of the ideas. Having picked myself up off the floor I pondered over the usefulness I have found continuity of names to be, and yet just how misleading can be quite simple name changes.

In East Cleveland lies the small village of North Skelton, a product of the growth of the ironstone mining industry in the area which had been sparked off by the discovery of a thick and workable seam at Eston in 1850.

Figure 1. The map shows the position of North Skelton in relation to the old village of Skelton. *Ordnance Survey maps of 1895 and 1930, scale 6 inches to the mile*

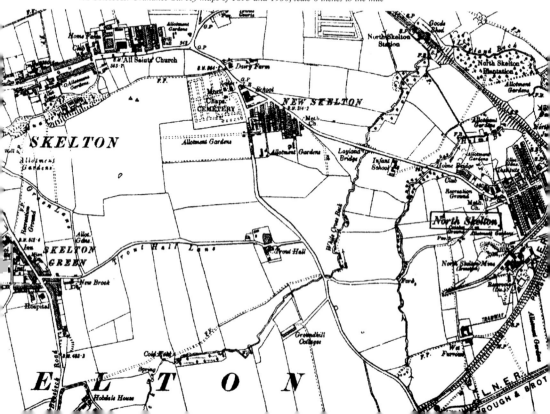

Mining villages of similar age and utility exist in the area, several denoted by the prefix 'New', in fact there is a 'New Skelton' but this is later in date than North Skelton and was built as several associated terraces of houses with odd shops in places, and never attained the status of even a village. So why 'North' Skelton when the place lies to the south- east of the pre-conquest village of Skelton (formerly known as Skelton-in-Cleveland) (Figure 1).

Prior to the realisation of the value and utility of Cleveland ironstone, the area had been tranquil and rural with several small ancient villages, widely spread, and farmsteads dotted about the landscape; not unlike, of course, much of the rest of rural Britain. However, one of the new fangled railways reached Guisborough in 1854, and another was extended in 1861 from the coastal town of Redcar to a planned seaside resort at a place called Saltburn. The Stockton and Darlington Railway was behind both schemes to achieve access into the anticipated ironstone mining area, whilst a distinct competitor, the Cleveland Railway, opened its line from the Skelton mine to the river Tees at Normanby, also in 1861.

Hard on the heels of the railway companies came several ironmasters with their various iron-making companies keen to exploit the ironstone known to exist in abundance in this new mining area. Generally in Cleveland, getting agreements to open mines was straightforward; as much of the land was held by major landowners keen to increase their income from what was to most an invisible asset.

Henry Bolckow, German by birth and an established businessman, formed a company with a well-known engineer, John Vaughan, and acquired successful collieries and ironworks. Their success at opening out the Eston mines under the direction of mining engineer and geologist, John Marley, had led them to establish more ironworks on the south bank of the Tees and with the general growth of iron-making encouraged them to look further afield for more supplies of ironstone.

From 1865 Messrs Bolckow, Vaughan & Company Limited leased a huge tract of land lying between Skelton and Brotton beneath which ironstone was known to exist, but exactly at what depth and extent were details needing to be investigated. Squire Wharton of Skelton Castle was the landowner from whom the company leased the area at a rent of £2,986 each year, payable whether any ironstone was produced or not. For this sum of money 134,370 tons of ironstone could be worked in any one year and if there should be output above this total, then for each additional ton worked a payment of 5d had to be made.

Obviously the company was anxious to commence mining in its newly leased area, or royalty; unfortunately, to move the mined ironstone a railway was needed and although during this same year the Cleveland Railway opened its new extension which crossed through the land in question, it was well to the south of where the ironstone seam could be expected to be deep underground and therefore expensive to reach. However, another railway was planned to be built from Saltburn (north of the royalty) southwards across it to join the Cleveland Railway and this was considered to be ideal for serving the intended mine. Soon after leaving Saltburn this railway would need to cross a wide and deep ravine which also marked the northern edge of the leased ground and here, John Marley, a mining engineer retained by the company, proposed to deal with the miner's great enemy, water. The valley was some 150 feet deep, the stream flowing through it providing the power for the nearby Marske Mill, so by commencing to drive a horizontal drift into the south side of the valley, just above stream level, Marley expected to be able to penetrate well into what was undoubtedly a very wet area of land and tap off some of this water. At the same time he also expected to be able to discover something of the quality and character of the ironstone.

Then came the bad news! The seam was nowhere to be found and instead the level had to be driven through thick, damp boulder clay, unpleasant to work in and even more unpleasant to have to pay for! During 1866 this drift was continued whilst boreholes were sunk ahead to find the ironstone and attempt to understand its nature. Not surprisingly, Messrs Bolckow and Vaughan were somewhat concerned at this and regular reports on progress were sent to the company's directors regarding their Skelton royalty. As this site of operations was at the north end it became referred to as North Skelton, a name that stuck, even when attention became focused on the center where shaft sinking commenced in 1869. The Main Seam of Cleveland ironstone was eventually found in the drift near Marske Mill which proved that in ancient geological times a huge valley had existed here and much of the seam had eroded away so any plans to mine it in the present valley were pointless.

The shaft sinking which had commenced in the center of the royalty in 1869 also stopped in 1869 at a depth of sixty feet when the inflow of water overcame progress. In fact the whole project was in peril, but the following year a new site was selected some 400 yards to the east in the yard of Foggo Farm and shaft sinking commenced again. It was to take some three years to reach the Main Seam at a depth of 720 feet after enormous difficulties coping with huge quantities of water.

To revert for a moment back to 1867, it would appear that the landowner was initially reluctant to allow the construction of cottages on his land that was leased to the iron company, but the need for them was urgent to house the group of men to be employed in shaft sinking. Fortunately, half a mile to the southwest was a long narrow strip of land owned by Groundhills Farm and leased to another iron company, Messrs Elwon. Agreement was reached during the year to build the necessary terrace of cottages here and it was subsequently named Elwon Terrace. Over the years the name of these isolated houses became changed to Groundhills Cottages, until they became empty and were demolished about 1960.

To return to the shaft sinking at North Skelton, the ironstone seam was reached 12 December 1873 and found to be free of water. The directors of Messrs Bolckow, Vaughan & Company Limited held their next monthly meeting on 18 December 1873 and to them there cannot have been a better Christmas present than this news, emphasized by the placing of a sample of the ironstone from the shaft bottom on the table in front of the meeting. Edward Williams was the general manager of the company and therefore partly responsible for the development of this difficult and lengthy mining venture, so a unanimous resolution was passed to award him a bonus of £1,000 (perhaps equivalent to £1 million today). Amid this general rejoicing came a report that a serious fire had occurred at the company's Longacres mine near to North Skelton, a much smaller sinking, but the damage was to be sufficient to delay it by two months.

With shafts sunk and permanent buildings under construction on the surface, it was necessary to begin constructing houses to accommodate the increasing workforce at this greenfield site. By March 1876, 234 miners were at work at North Skelton mine, (Figure 2) with perhaps a similar number employed as deputies, haulage hands, bricklayers, engineers etc. William Armstrong, an independent mining engineer, reported to the company in September 1876 that 176 cottages in the adjoining new village were built and occupied and that fifty more were in hand.

It was this new community clustered around the new mine that

Figure 2. The map shows the street names and the position of the North Skelton Mine. *Extract from Ordnance Survey map of 1894 scale 1:2500.*

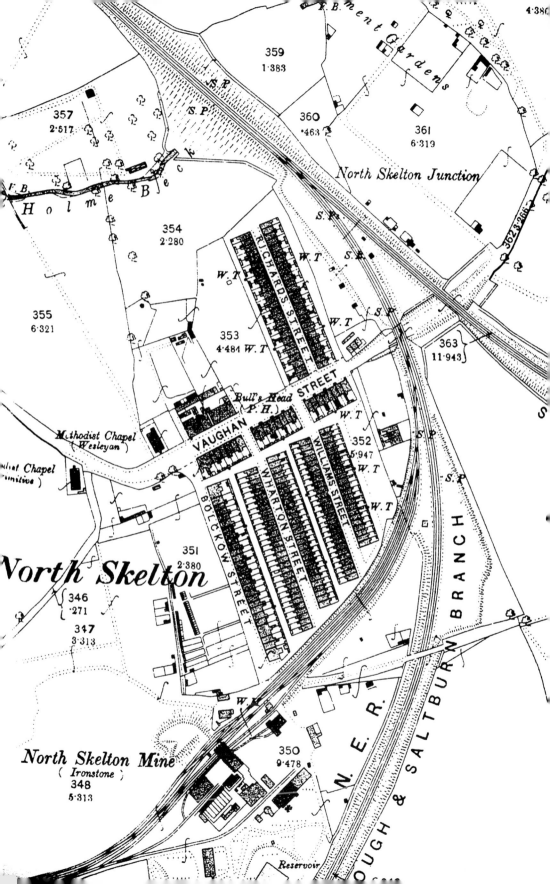

obviously adopted the name which had become applied to the mining activities in the royalty, and so the village became North Skelton. In due time a chapel, a meeting room, shops, a public house and institute were erected. As the village was largely owned by Messrs Bolckow and Vaughan, they also named the streets. Running approximately east to west was the main street, the high road from Skelton to Brotton and this was called, appropriately, Vaughan Street. One of the first terraces to be built must have been on the east side of the lane running uphill from this main road to the mine site and this was called Bolckow Street. The street built next, to the east and parallel to Bolckow Street, was named after the landowner as Wharton Street. Next again to the east was room for a further street which was named Williams Street, after the man who had been in charge of the company during the very difficult and costly period of developing this mine, Edward Williams, the general manager.

Edward Williams retired during 1875 but was in communication with the company at the year-end regarding the non-payment of £1,000 to which he believed he was entitled. The company replied that this sum had been voted to him annually as a performance bonus and was not given as a right. His successor was Arthur Windsor Richards as general manager and what better way to welcome him than to name the latest street in North Skelton after him. Hence, Richards Street was built to the north of Vaughan Street, as land was no longer available to the south.

In general terms, North Skelton changed little over the years except for the building of St Peter's Church, the working men's club and several houses along the main road leading towards the village of Skelton. North Skelton railway station was opened, then closed again many years later. North Skelton Mine achieved fame as the last Cleveland ironstone mine to remain at work, but it eventually closed on 17 January 1964. Since then further houses have been added to the west end of the village but fortunately the street names of the original village remain as a reminder of the origins of this small community. However, this is not quite correct as Williams has become a first name, so has Richards. New nameplates put up in recent years display these streets to be William Street and Richard Street so could trap the unwary historian in future years into putting a whole new meaning into their use.

There is no disputing the origins and purpose of the village of Liverton Mines, its name is self explanatory, although unusual, even in Cleveland. Several similar villages came into being around the same time for the same reason, the opening of an ironstone mine and the necessity to create a village for the miners and their families. New Marske and New Brotton also speak for themselves, although the latter is now very reduced in size from its original creation. But why was Liverton Mines first called New London?

For the answer to this we need to look at the initial establishment of a mine in this location in 1866. John Watson appears to have been an entrepreneur, perhaps with businesses in Whitby, the Esk Valley and London. Having realised the potential for making money out of the ironstone mining boom post-1850, he appears to have done the donkey work of determining which areas of land had potential for mineral exploitation, who the landowners were and what leases they favoured for mining. Having arranged all this, and perhaps even taking up a mining lease himself, he then sold this on to another individual or company to exploit whilst making for himself what we can assume would be a handsome profit.

Lord Downe, in the 1860s owned a large tract of land south of the town of Lofthouse and enclosing the tiny village of Liverton. Watson obtained a lease to mine beneath this area in 1865. Next comes the dodgy bit!

It was a practice, common in lead and other metalliferous mining to obtain mining leases in remote areas e.g. Wales or Yorkshire, especially in the vicinity of existing successful mines, and to encourage investment in mining them among the well-off and keen investors of London. Much money could be invested by people fed on regular enthusiastic reports from the mines without their ability to check their accuracy. Some people lost huge sums of money this way and Watson's activities lead to suspicions that he may have been acting in a similar way, but definite evidence is lacking. However, we do know that in 1866, Watson sold his mining interest in Lord Downe's Liverton estate to Sir Charles Fox and Peter Graham, both of London. Between them they formed the Liverton Ironstone Company Limited in 1865, the necessary capital of £24,000 being raised through shares being taken up by four members of the Graham family and three of the Fox's, proof if it were needed, of their wealth. Peter Graham appears to have been a self made businessman, whilst Sir Charles Fox had been knighted for his part in building the Great Exhibition building in 1851, better known as the Crystal Palace.

A branch of the Cleveland Railway, passing over the 150 feet high

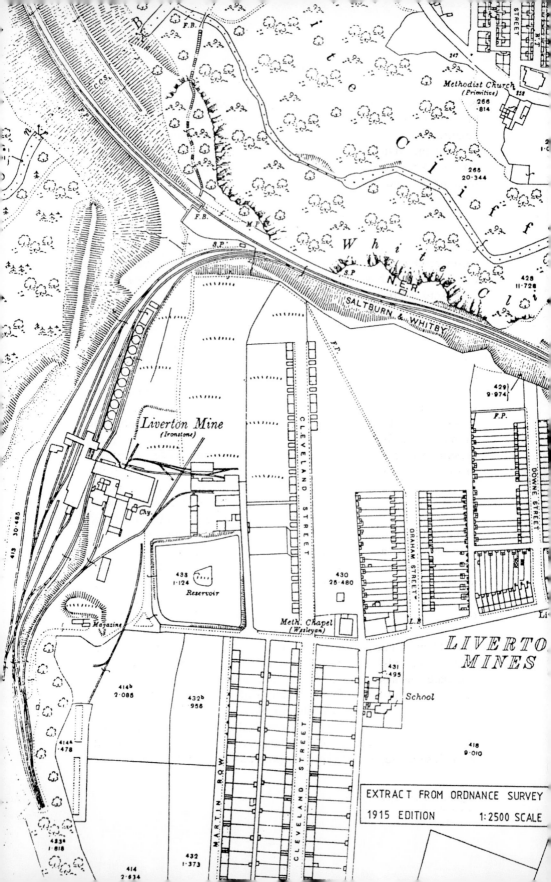

EXTRACT FROM ORDNANCE SURVEY
1915 EDITION   1:2500 SCALE

Kilton Viaduct, was opened to Lofthouse in 1867 and work soon began on sinking two shafts for the new mine in the Liverton royalty (Figure 3). The first output was recorded in 1871 after the shafts had reached the Main Seam at a depth of 480 feet. The capital needed quickly exceeded the original amount subscribed so further shares were issued and again taken up by the two families, although this time many more relatives were involved. On this greenfield site everything had to be provided, so the first terraces of houses were soon erected for the workforce. I suspect that initially, they may have been of wooden construction and single storey; certainly single storey brick houses were built in Martin Row and Cleveland Street, the northern section of Cleveland Street being demolished around 1900 through being unfit for habitation.

The Liverstone Ironstone Company was about the only one formed in the Cleveland mining field where all the founders came from London. This is the reason why the new settlement became known as 'New London' and is recorded as such by the 1871 census. Francis Fox, Sir Charles' second son, aged twenty-eight in 1872, was appointed as a manager at the mine in the same year by Peter Graham, chairman of the company, 'not so much a mining engineer as someone he could trust to report everything to the directors'. Francis, with his wife and young child lived in Saltburn and presumably he commuted to work by horse as it was to be 1875 before a railway station was to be opened at Lofthouse. As the North Eastern Railway Company already had another Lofthouse Station in the West Riding of Yorkshire, to avoid confusion, the new one was called Loftus, no doubt based on the local pronunciation of the town name.

In one of his autobiographies, Francis was very proud of the fact that he designed some of the more conventional double storey terraced houses which comprise Graham and Downe Streets, and also Cliffe Terrace, so we can assume they were built from 1873 onwards. Obviously the first street was named in honour of the company chairman, Peter Graham, the next after the landowner, Lord Downe. Francis Fox had a very patriarchal influence over the village which his family had helped to establish; perhaps he and his associates always referred to the place as the mines at Liverton, or Liverton mines, which could explain how the name survived while New London eventually fell out of use.

The Liverton ironstone mines did well in the early 1870s when trade generally was buoyant but the decline starting in 1875 caused it to close in August 1877, leaving the much respected Francis Fox

Figure 3. The map shows the position of the Liverton Mine. *Extract from Ordnance Survey map of 1915, scale 1:2500.*

to bemoan in his latter years of the great amount of money that had been lost at the time. Knighted for his part in devising the elaborate scheme which prevented the collapse of Winchester Cathedral between 1906 and 1912, he died in 1927.

Liverton Mines reopened for six months in 1880 under new management, and was the bought by the Cargo Fleet Iron Company Limited in 1882. Captain John George Swan, chairman of the company, exercised the same degree of paternalism over the mine and village until his death in 1900; for example his company was in the habit of paying each man who worked between Christmas and New Year each year a bonus of half a crown (12.5p now). Afterwards the company was taken over by the business empire of Baron Furness and a major development of the mine undertaken in 1903. But things were never the same and when Cargo Fleet Iron Company began to lose money dramatically, in early 1921 the mine was closed. Fortunately with the availability of work at other local mines and Skinningrove Iron and Steel Works, unreliable as it was, the village stayed alive and was expanded with post-war council house building. However, the mine did reopen during the 1950s when passages were driven through underground into the abandoned workings from the adjoining Kilton Mine and further ironstone was extracted for a few years via the Kilton shafts until that mine closed in 1963.

Like so many similar, small settlements, Liverton Mines has a proud and fascinating, if perhaps short history worthy of further study.

4. THE WRECK OF THE 'BIRGER': A TRUE STORY OF GREAT HEROISM AND CRUEL TRAGEDY

by Gary Green

EIGHTEENTH OF OCTOBER 1898 SAW THE EVENTS of one of the most dramatic and tragic shipwrecks ever witnessed along the North-East coast of England brought to a heart rending close, as the Finnish sailing vessel Birger struck the Saltscar Rocks at Redcar and was wrecked with the loss of thirteen of her fifteen-man crew. Just over 100 years later, a team of local scuba divers recovered one of the vessel's large anchors from the wreck site. Carefully conserved, this anchor now stands at the Kirkleatham Museum, Redcar, where it serves as a powerful and permanent memorial to the thirteen courageous crewmen who lost their lives on that tragic day. This then, is the story of the *Birger*.

The Final Voyage

In late September 1898, the large Finnish barque *Birger* began what was to be her final and most dramatic voyage. She sailed from San Felieu de Guixols, a small port some fifty miles north of Barcelona, bound for Abo (modern day Turku) in Finland with a cargo of salt. She was under the command of thirty-five year-old Captain Karl Nordling with a crew of fourteen seamen, all of them Russian Finns and with an average age of just twenty.

The *Birger's* course (Figure 1) would take her through the Straits of Gibraltar, northwards across the Bay of Biscay through the English Channel and then up the North Sea towards her final destination in the Baltic. However, before she had even left the Mediterranean, while off the North African coast she sprang a leak. It would seem the leak was not too serious as it was successfully brought under control and the barque continued on her voyage without having to make port for repairs. The remainder of the voyage passed without further incident until she approached the Norwegian coast. Here she was struck by a ferocious storm from the north, a storm that was to last for five days. Unable to make any headway against the gale force winds, the *Birger* was driven back down the North Sea, her hull being so worked and strained that the leak she sustained in the Mediterranean was reopened and she began to take on water. When somewhere near the Dogger Bank, Captain Nordling

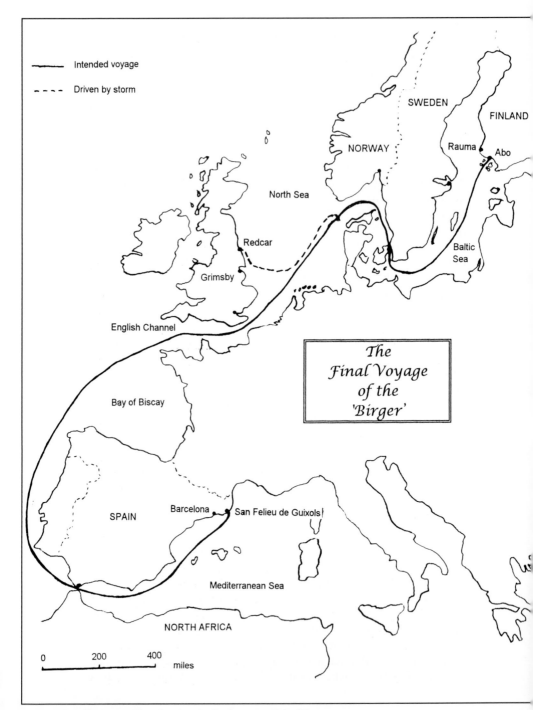

Figure 1. Map showing the final voyage of the *Birger*. *Author's collection*

decided to run his ship for the shelter of Grimsby, one of the first ports visited by the barque nearly thirty years earlier and the course was set. However, when nearing the English coast the wind began to veer to a more southeasterly direction and Captain Nordling decided instead to make for Newcastle.

In gale force south-easterly winds and driving rain, the slowly sinking barque made landfall at Scarborough, where to all who watched from the shore, it seemed inevitable that she must come ashore. The crew of the Scarborough Lifeboat *Queensbury* was assembled and the boat speedily launched. The local Life Saving Rocket Brigade was also quickly on the scene. However, neither was needed. With superb seamanship the battered vessel was steered clear of the land and passed rapidly up the coast. The lifeboat was quickly recalled when it became clear that it could not hope to catch the storm driven barque and though the Rocket Brigade cart pursued the barque for some time along the coast road northwards, it too was soon obliged to give up the chase and return to the station.

By now, news of the barque's plight had been passed along the coast ahead of her, alerting other lifeboat stations of the distressed vessel's approach. The Robin Hood's Bay, Whitby and Saltburn lifeboats were all prepared, though in the event they were not called upon to attempt a rescue. Shortly after midday, the crowd lining the cliffs at Robin Hood's Bay saw the vessel loom out of the murk, clearly in trouble and flying signals of distress. With the sea too rough for the lifeboat to launch, the people of the Bay could only watch helplessly as first a topsail and then a storm-sail split and were blown to ribbons, seemingly leaving the *Birger* at the mercy of the storm.

Driven ever northwards it was not long before the *Birger* was sighted approaching Whitby Harbour and again the local lifeboat was at the ready. However, the state of the seas made it impossible for the barque to enter the port safely and Captain Nordling had little choice but to head back out to sea and seek safety elsewhere. Somehow and with quite remarkable courage and seamanship, Captain Nordling and his cold, exhausted crew had managed to keep their vessel afloat, though by now the hull was waterlogged and with most of the sails blown away the vessel was nearly unmanageable.

At around 1.00 pm, the virtually drifting barque was sighted off Staithes. Once again, Captain Nordling, realising that it would be impossible to try and enter that tiny harbour, kept his vessel away from the shore only just clearing the cliffs at Skinningrove and Huntcliff. As the barque reached Saltburn the end now seemed very near. Passing close to the end of Saltburn Pier, the *Birger* was soon caught in the breakers, surely now about to be driven ashore. The lifeboat Mary Hatcher was crewed and ready to be launched the instant the vessel struck. Yet, incredibly, the crew of the *Birger* managed to turn her head once more to seawards and somehow she clawed her way back out to sea. Such magnificent seamanship and determination deserved to be rewarded with better, but it was not to be. At Redcar the drama drew to a finale.

At a little after 2.00 pm, the people of Redcar saw the *Birger* hove into sight. Realising he was heading straight for the 1,200 foot long Redcar Pier, Captain Nordling again put his sinking barque's head to seaward. Carrying all of what little sail she had left, with her rigging in tatters and her decks constantly swept by huge seas, the barque narrowly missed the head of the pier and headed out to sea. But her luck had run out.

Lying between his vessel and the open sea lay the Redcar rocks, a notorious reef stretching over one and a half miles out to sea. The unfortunate *Birger*, by now waterlogged and barely afloat, was simply unable to weather this last obstacle and she crashed headlong onto the Saltscar rocks.

Within a few minutes both the Fore and Mizzenmasts came crashing down, killing the gallant Captain Nordling and his Chief Officer. Pounded by huge waves the ill-fated barque quickly began to break up. Almost as soon as the vessel struck, the Royal National Lifeboat *Brothers* was launched, followed shortly afterwards by the older and smaller fisherman's lifeboat *Emma*. Such was the violence of the seas that the lighter boat *Emma* was unable to make any progress and was fortunate not to be dashed to pieces herself against the Coatham Pier before being thrown back on the beach by the huge breakers.

The *Brothers* meanwhile, after a desperate struggle through the now mountainous seas, slowly began to make headway to where the *Birger* was rapidly going to pieces. Heavy seas and the enormous tangle of wreckage being washed about prevented the lifeboat from closing in on the wreck. Having searched the area for some time in great peril themselves, the crew of the lifeboat had little choice but to return to shore, greatly saddened and disappointed that they had been unable to save any lives and fearing that all hands had been lost.

However, the spectators who lined the nearby Coatham Pier watching the dramatic rescue attempts unfold, observed through the flying spray, three of the barque's crew drifting towards them on a large piece of wreckage. As this wreckage was driven through the iron legs of the pier, ropes were lowered down to the men, one of whom managed to take a turn of rope around his arm and shouted to be hauled up. Numbed with cold and virtually exhausted, the unfortunate crewman could not hold on and was swept away by the waves. The remaining two men were by now clinging to the pier leg tie-rods and again ropes were lowered down to them. Huge waves quickly washed one man to his death, however the other, Emil Nordstrom, managed to hold on just long enough to be pulled over the pier railings to safety. A little further along the beach a second survivor, Johan Makila, was dragged to safety from the clutches of the breakers by some of the willing members of the large crowd that had assembled to render what assistance they could. As the tragedy of the shipwreck drew to a close, it was realised with shock and horror that only two of the fifteen crew had survived (Figure 2). Yet

Figure 2. Johan Makila and Emil Nordstom, the only two young men to survive the last voyage of the *Birger*. *Kirkleatham Old Hall Museum*

Figure 3. Coatham Pier with part of the structure and the middle pavilion cut off from the landward end. The damage was caused by the wreckage of the Birger driving into the pier during the storm of 18 October 1898. *Kirkleatham Old Hall Museum*

the drama was not over. The large crowd of people lining Coatham Pier suddenly realised they themselves were in now in great danger. The heavy piece of wreckage from which Emil Nordstrom had been plucked to safety was now being driven like a battering ram against the pier legs. With a shout of warning, the crowds made a mad scramble to the safety of the shore and not a moment too soon as a weakened section of the pier, fifty yards long, collapsed and crashed into the raging surf. Fortunately no one was hurt (Figure 3).

In the days following the disaster, the bodies of the unfortunate crewmen began to be washed ashore and were buried in three local cemeteries, Christ Church, Coatham, St Germains, Marske and Holy Trinity, Seaton Carew. Great sorrow was felt in the town of Redcar and this sorrow was deepened when Christmas gifts the crew were taking home to their families began washing up onto the beach. Local people were moved to put pen to paper as in this contemporary poem commemorating the loss of the barque and her crew (Figure 4).

Figure 4. The local Redcar residents with some of the wreckage of a wooden sailing ship, believed to be that of the Birger. *Kirkleatham Old Hall Museum*

The Wreck of the *Birger*

On the eighteenth day of October
In the year eighteen ninety eight
A fearful gale from the E.S.East
Brought a Russian barque in sight

•

She drifted along the North East coast
It was then half past two o'clock
Lost to view in the sea almost
Till she pitched on Saltscar Rock

•

The sea was tossing mountains high
And swept everything off the deck
It was then very plain to be seen
The vessel would soon be a wreck

•

A cry went aloud 'Launch the lifeboat'
And was echoed by one and all
That was standing on the foreshore
Ready to assist any call

•

It had not been very long sounded
Before the lifeboat was afloat
When willing workers with ropes did pull
And bravely launched the gallant boat

•

Soon the second lifeboat was ordered
And launched with the same success
They are not half-hearted working men
When poor sailors are in distress

•

All praise is due to the lifeboat men
Who struggled hard with all their might
And battled against the raging sea
As we watched them out of sight

•

They pulled till they were exhausted
So anxious were they to save
Those fifteen hardy Russian sailors
From death and a watery grave

•

Though their efforts were of no avail
They did everything that they could
For the storm had torn down mast and sail
And the sea near was covered with wood

•

Night was then coming on them amain
As they headed their boat to land
It seemed hopeless looking again
For drowned must be every hand

•

God's Will was that it should not be so
Only He can rule o'er the sea
And can call on the waves to let go
Saying give up my people to me

•

Shortly after was seen through a glass
Seven men clinging to a raft
Then two of them were seen to pass
Leaving five only on the frail craft

•

Two more were washed into the sea
Every heart was filled with fear
Three only remained, only three
And they cast up to Coatham Pier

•

Ropes were soon lowered down off the pier
For the poor young men to take hold
And they grasped with a death like fear
Though their hands were benumbed with cold

•

One fell back into the raging sea
And was not seen to rise anymore
A sight that will long remembered be
By all those that stood on the shore

•

Another one clung onto some more wreck
In hopes for his life to save
Whilst a man waded up to his neck
And clutched him out from the wild wave

•

Thus two of the men have been saved
And three lifeless bodies found

Fine looking young men, well behaved
We all wish them well when homebound

The three left behind have been buried
Amidst every token of respect
On the shoulder's of strangers carried
And their graves with flowers bedecked

They are laid to rest at Coatham
In the graveyard by the sea
Not far from where the waves cast them
May they long remembered be.

By Allan Wardill
54 High Street Redcar

And so onto the final, or perhaps just the latest chapter in the *Birger* story. In the summer of 1983, I received a phone call from a good friend of mine, Jimmy Dick, inviting me out for a dive (Figure 5). Jimmy was a professional North Sea diver and had been asked by a local fisherman if he would recover a line, or beat of crab pots that had become snagged on some underwater obstruction or other. Usually this meant the pot-ropes had wrapped themselves round an outcrop of rock, but occasionally they were caught up in a wreck - and in wrecks we were very definitely interested!

As we loaded our equipment into the fishing boat it was very nearly a perfect day for diving, blue sky, light winds and the promise

Figure 5. Jimmy Dick and Gary Green, the divers who discovered the wreck site. *Author's collection*

of good 'viz' i.e. clear underwater visibility. The pots lay in shallow water almost in the middle of a triangle formed by the wrecks of the Dimitris Fairplay 11 and the High Stone rocks (Figure 6). As we entered the water and adjusted our diving gear we could see, looking down from the surface, the dappled sunlight bouncing off the rocky seabed below. This meant excellent underwater visibility.

Acting as Jimmy's 'dive buddy' my task was simply to keep an eye on him while he sorted out the tangle of pots and ropes – after all he was the professional diver! Following him down the rope we soon discovered that the pots had become entangled around a very large Admiralty-pattern anchor standing almost upright on the seabed. Now this was interesting! However we, or rather Jimmy, had a job to do and it was straight down to business. Untangling the cat's cradle of pots and ropes was a tricky business and led inevitably to steadily deteriorating visibility as we inadvertently stirred up sand and sediments.

By the time we were finished, visibility in the immediate area had been reduced to a couple of feet and Jimmy was now running short of air. Nevertheless we just had sufficient time for a quick look around and through the now very murky water were able to make out other pieces of wreckage lying close to the anchor. All too soon it was time to surface. Once back in the boat, we exchanged broad grins, this was a site we just had to come back to.

The following week we returned, this time purely to dive on and examine the wreckage. The 'viz' was still good and with each of us armed with a tape measure, dive slate and pencil we began to take measurements, draw sketches and take notes of all we saw. What we found convinced us that we had stumbled across the remains of the bows of a large wooden sailing vessel.

The wreckage was lying on a fairly flat and nondescript area of rock interspersed with a few patches of sand, the only feature of any note being a low oval shaped mound of small rocks and boulders. Sitting on top of this mound was a large Admiralty-pattern anchor nearly twelve feet long, the one that had originally snagged the crab pots. Swimming closer we could see this anchor was actually standing over not one, but two further anchors, both lying flat amongst a mass of rusting anchor chain. One was actually a little larger than the upright anchor, while the other was only half the size. Not only that, where this anchor chain and other iron fittings had corroded and combined with particles of sand and small stones, it had formed concretions. Set within these concretions were various items of ship's rigging such as wooden blocks and deadeyes. We could

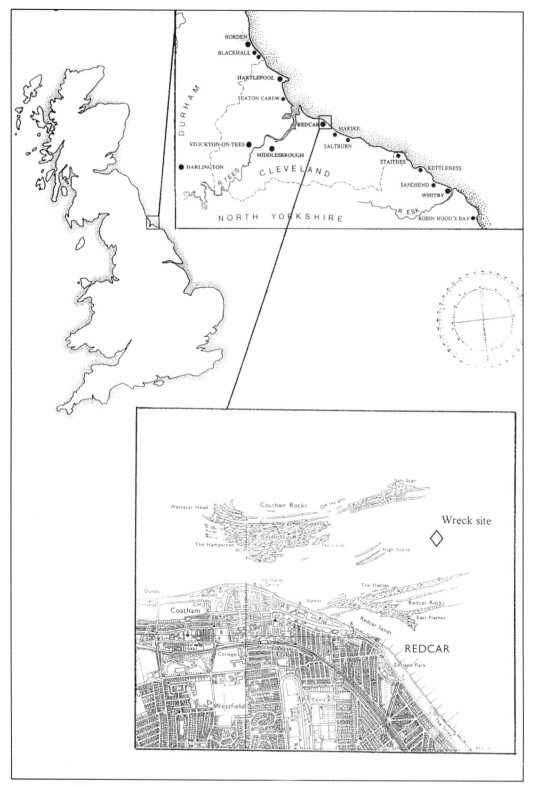

Figure 6. Map of location and wreck site. *Author's collection*

also see lying just a short distance from the anchors an iron capstan and the remains of a windlass, both of which would have been used in raising and lowering the vessel's anchors.

Slightly further away lay a ten-foot long section of the vessel's wooden keel. This was a very substantial piece of timber over twelve inches (30 cm) square and still with pieces of yellow metal (brass) sheathing attached. In addition, scattered over the whole area of the wreck site were a number of smaller items such as a sounding lead, a section of lead scupper pipe and a long brass nail or bolt, just one of many used to fasten the ribs of the vessel to the keel. We recovered some of these smaller items in the hope that they might provide us with clues as to the identity of the ship, though unfortunately they did not. As they required little in the way of conservation treatment we were soon able to put them on display in the Zetland Lifeboat Museum, Redcar, where they can still be seen today. Having recorded as much as we could of the wreckage, Jimmy and I then explored the surrounding area for any other traces of the wreck, though without success. In the language of the sea, this ship had very quickly and very literally 'gone to pieces', leaving only these few heavy items on the seabed to mark her grave.

But what was this vessel? How had she been wrecked and when? It was now time to turn detective and this was where I became the expert. Having always had a deep interest in shipwrecks, particularly local wrecks, I had over the years collected quite an assortment of books, charts and newspaper cuttings on the subject and it was to these that I now turned to for clues. Redcar rocks and in particular the Saltscar rock, have taken a terrible toll of ships and their crews; positively identifying 'our' wreck would not be easy. However it was to be the very size of the wreckage that would prove to be the key to this mystery. Put simply, large vessels carried large anchors, the two 'twelve footers' on our wreck site clearly belonged to a large vessel.

Looking through my records, I found two vessels that had been lost on Redcar rocks both of which were large enough to have carried such substantial anchors. One of these vessels was an American barque, the Stonewall Jackson, which was wrecked in 1883 in calm weather, on rocks a little to the north of the anchor site. This vessel had been extensively salvaged and it seemed likely that such easily accessible items as the anchors and rigging blocks would have been recovered as a matter of course. This then was not our wreck. The other large vessel known to be lost here was the *Birger*.

Researching a shipwreck requires a great deal of time and effort, particularly if the vessel is of foreign nationality and records are hard to find. As the *Birger* was Finnish, I made enquiries to the Finnish National Maritime Museum and the local museum in the barque's home port of Rauma. This produced a wealth of information and details of the *Birger*'s history.

A Brief History

The *Birger* was a wooden barque, (Figure 7) built in Pateniemi, Finland towards the end of 1869 and completed early the following year. She was a large vessel of 736 tons and measured 163 feet long (54.5m) with a beam of 34 feet (10.3m) and a depth of hold of 22 feet (5.9m). She was a well-built vessel designed for long ocean voyages and her bottom was sheathed in yellow metal (brass). A part translated builder's inventory details the cost of the materials used in the construction of the vessel. Many items are listed, ranging from deck beams, planks and pitch, to twine, tallow and even green paint. Provisions for the vessel included thirteen pots of rum, thirty pots of schnapps, as well as sugar, bread, butter and fish. The final bill from the shipyard came to just under 122,000 Finnish marks, which, in the present day would be about £12,000 in British currency, a fairly expensive vessel.

Between 1870 and 1895, the vessel was owned by the commercial house G & C Bergbom (or Bergholm), in Oulu and that certainly by

Figure 7. The barque *Birger* as she looked when she was built. *Kirkleatham Old Hall Museum*

1873 she was insured with the Finnish Sea Insurance Company for 120,000 marks. Detailed accounts of her voyages are scarce, however it seems likely that her maiden voyage was in fact to Grimsby, the port that unwittingly had a bearing on the *Birger*'s tragic final loss.

In her early voyages she regularly visited New York, Liverpool, Kronstadt and her home port of Oulu. Other ports of call included Havana, New Orleans, Hamburg and Philadelphia. In 1876 she arrived in Antwerp with a cargo of wheat, having been badly damaged in a storm. In 1885 she sailed from Sharpness bound for New York under the command of J A Laurin and in December 1888, she was again back in New York. In 1895 she was sold to Captain Karl Oscar Nordling and a consortium of other merchants in Rauma for 25,000 marks and at the not inconsiderable age for a sailing ship of twenty-five years, continued her trade.

Three years later, in September 1898, the barque sailed on her final, fateful voyage (Figure 8).

Research nearer to home had put me in touch with an ex-patriot Finn living in Redcar, Mr Len Pippo. Len had discovered a large and impressive memorial stone still standing in Coatham churchyard, dedicated to the unfortunate crew. Close by was a smaller headstone marking the grave of a single crewmember.

Figure 8. The crew of the Birger before she set sail from Spain. The photo was distributed as a postcard. *Kirkleatham Old Hall Museum*

The following are the inscriptions on each of the four sides of the stone:

On the north face:

SACRED

TO THE MEMORY

OF CAPT KARL OSCAR NORDLING

OF RAUMO

FINLAND

AGED 35

AND TWELVE OF THE CREW

OF THE BARQUE *BIRGER*

OF RAUMO

WHO WERE DROWNED IN THE

WRECK OF THAT VESSEL AT

REDCAR ON OCT 18TH 1898

GUSTAF BENCTSSON BOIJER

AGED 19

GUSTAF FREDRIK FORSLOF

AGED 20

GUSTAF FREDRIK LINDROOS

AGED 21

WHO ARE BURIED IN THIS

CHURCHYARD

On the south face:

ALSO

KARL ARVID SILVENDOINEEN

MATE

AGE 34

ERNST EDVART ELONEN

AGE 20

JOSEF AUGUST MATTSONSVEN

AGE 19

WHOSE BODIES WERE NOT IDENTIFIED

On the east face:

IN THIS GRAVE

REST THE BODIES OF

GUSTAF BENCTSSON BOIJER

OF BJORNBORG

FINLAND

AGED 19

AND

GUSTAF FREDRIK LINDROOS

OF RAUMO, FINLAND
AGED 21
JESU MERCY

On the west face:

ALSO
EMIL ARTUR ARVONEN
AGED 18
WILKO WILK
AGED 34
WHO ARE BURIED IN MARSKE
GUSTAF LUDVIG FOGELMAN
AGED 18
JOHAN NESTOR JOKILA
AGED 19
ZACHARIAS SALONEN
AGED 25
WHO ARE BURIED IN SEATON CAREW

Around the base of the stone are the following inscriptions:
THE WAVES OF THE SEA ARE MIGHTY AND RAGE
HORRIBLY BUT YET THE LORD WHO DWELLETH
ON HIGH IS MIGHTIER and MAKE THEM TO BE
NUMBERED WITH THY SAINTS IN
GLORY EVERLASTING

The smaller single gravestone has the following inscription:

GUSTAF FREDRIK FORSLOF
OF RAUMO FINLAND
BORN 1878
DECEASED OCTOBER 18 1898
JESU MERCY

Further enquiries revealed that the bodies of four of the crew had been washed up at Seaton Carew some five miles north of Redcar and on the other side of the river Tees. A large headstone marks their grave in the cemetery of Holy Trinity Church, Seaton Carew and bears the following inscription:

THE BODIES OF
ZACHARIAS SALONEN

OF LAPPI FINLAND
AGED 25 YEARS
JOHAN NESTOR JOKILA
OF RAUMO FINLAND
AGED 18 YEARS
GUSTAF LUDWIG FOGELMAN
OF RAUMO FINLAND
AGED 18 YEARS
AND ANOTHER WHO WAS NOT IDENTIFIED
ALL OF WHOM WERE DROWNED IN THE
WRECK OF THE BARQUE "*BIRGER*"
AT REDCAR OCTOBER 18TH 1898
JESU MERCY

And there for the next fifty years the story stopped. Jimmy found less and less time to dive for 'fun' and even though I had joined a local diving club, Cleveland Divers, my 'club' dives were rarely anywhere near the wreck site. However, all this was to change after a club dive in 1998. The dive organiser suggested the anchor site would make a good 'second dive' for a number of new club members who had not visited the site before and he thought it might be 'quite interesting' for them. Indeed it was. With the centenary of the *Birger*'s loss fast approaching, from this one dive grew a club project that would ultimately see the large, upright anchor raised from the seabed and sited at the Kirkleatham Hall Museum Redcar. Here it would form a truly impressive memorial to the courageous crew of the *Birger* who lost their lives on that dreadful day in October 1898. But that was not all. Everyone involved in the project felt that while it was very important to look back and remember the tragedy, it was also important to look forward and to this end the anchor was to form the centerpiece of a new maritime heritage display, based on the museum's varied collection of other locally recovered anchors.

The actual raising of the anchor from the seabed and its transportation to the shore was to be carried out by the Cleveland Divers. The theory was simple, we would attach a one-ton lifting bag plus six plastic drums at various points on the anchor, fill them with air and bring the anchor gently to the surface. Once at the surface and fully secured, it was to be towed to shore and at high water gently beached alongside the lifeboat slipway. When the tide had dropped sufficiently, the bag and drums would be removed and on the following day a crane would lift the anchor onto a lorry for the short journey to Kirkleatham Hall Museum. The whole project was to be video-recorded by two club members.

The reality, while more complicated than difficult, proved to be a major logistical effort involving the support and enthusiasm of a wide range of people and organizations. It was a credit to everyone who took part that the whole recovery operation went without a hitch.

The day of the lift dawned fine and clear, with just a light southwesterly breeze and a calm sea. This was to be a major club effort, involving the use of three boats, no less than seventeen divers and a substantial shore party. This shore party, while not only providing a point of contact for the press and many passers by who stopped to find out what was going on, also (and more importantly for the divers) supplied much needed bacon sandwiches and hot coffee throughout the day! By lunchtime the anchor was at the surface and a slow, gentle tow to the beach began. In fact the recovery had gone so smoothly that we had to wait a few hours for the tide to rise sufficiently to allow us to position the anchor alongside the slipway. By eight o'clock that evening the anchor had been safely beached and all the ropes, drums and lifting bag removed, it was time for a well-deserved beer.

Early the following morning a crane (a huge traffic stopping crane!) arrived on Redcar seafront where a sizeable crowd of people had gathered to watch the anchor being lifted onto a lorry for its final journey to the museum. Here the Curator, Phil Philo, had very kindly arranged for the anchor to undergo essential conservation to prevent it becoming a one and a half ton pile of rust! Following a lengthy treatment and a final coating of rust inhibitor, the anchor was moved to its final position in the museum grounds. And there it proudly stands today, a truly fitting and impressive memorial to the thirteen extremely brave and courageous crewmen who tragically lost their lives in the wreck of the barque *Birger* on 18 October 1898.

Acknowledgements

My good friend Jimmy Dick, without whose timely invitation to go diving the *Birger* story might have never been written; the membership of Cleveland Divers for recovering the anchor as a very fitting memorial to the lost crew; Phil Philo and the staff of Kirkleatham Old Hall Museum, Redcar, for their valuable support in the conservation and subsequent displaying of the anchor; Mike Poole of Initial GWS Cranes Ltd, for the extremely generous donation of a giant crane; Decosol Ltd of Sheffield for their valuable contribution of rust inhibitor; all the staff of the various Libraries and Museums who greatly assisted me in my research; the Finnish Maritime Museum for supplying invaluable information on the construction and history of the *Birger*; Mr Len Pippo, an expatriate Finn, for rediscovering and tending with dignity the graves of the crew in Coatham Churchyard; and not least, my wife Claire for patiently advising and proof reading my many rewrites of this fascinating, yet tragic story.

5. MONKEY BUSINESS: NOT AT ALL NAPOLEONIC

by Paul Screeton

FOR THOSE WHO KNOW ANYTHING at all about Hartlepool's monkey-hanging legend, popular perception has it reduced to a tale of simple fisher folk mistaking a washed-ashore monkey for a French spy and taking the expeditious measure of hanging the creature. The story is not unique to Hartlepool, but a little known sub-plot is specifically Hartlepudlian. That much of the subsequent detail can only be understood through reference to a bitter railways rivalry that is the subject of my thesis. Apart from the wretched simian and its tormentors, we will see how a multi-located legend spawned a specialized local frisson, where feelings ran high centuries ago and reverberate to this day.

Stranger on the Shore
During the Napoleonic Wars, a large French privateer, *Chasse Maree*, was spotted during a lift in the weather, passing close to Hartlepool's Headland. Shortly afterwards the ship struck the notorious Longscar rocks and broke up. Among the pieces of wreckage washed ashore was a spar, upon which clung a bedraggled, shivering monkey.

Chattering away and dressed in military style uniform, as was and still is a common practice for ship's pets, a Fish Sands 'lobster pot court martial' declared the poor beast should be hanged. The fishermen were not being simply ignorant, for there was a certain logic in taking such a precaution.

Strangely, none of the histories of Hartlepool at the time record this event, either as historical fact or folklore, for example the huge publicity for the fabled Lambton Worm, for surely had the hanging taken place it would have been the highpoint of events during Napoleonic times.

Railway Mania
Speaking volumes by its absence, the historian must press forward to the 1840s to find the earliest publication regarding monkeylore. Here a tantalizing reference is made in a political pamphlet to 'aquatic monkies'. The newly developed South East Durham coalfield needed good port facilities to transport its riches and by the early 1830s a serious plan had been mooted to improve facilities at

Hartlepool. As each relied upon the other, the undertaking took the name Hartlepool Dock and Railway Company. Opening in 1835, it became an immediate success, with ships able to enter, load and sail on the same tide.

A rival scheme brought a line curving from the south to Hartlepool, but whereas the former's coal was dropped from High Staithes, the newcomer's wagons had to be drawn up from the wharves at Throston Engine House. Shareholders of the Stockton and Hartlepool Railway sought to circumvent the costly engine house fee by creating their own dock. This act of aggression was to bring about the birth of West Hartlepool.

When in 1844, with the Stockton and Hartlepool Railway Bill before Parliament, the new proprietors across the lake, known as The Slake, found themselves having to contend with a surly local population, unhappy at the destruction of their historic and romantic moorings, threat to self reliance without elected authority and the misbehavior of the immigrant navvies.

Aquatic Monkies

A campaign to enlist the goodwill of the fishermen then got underway, for there is evidence from a pamphlet dated 8 February 1844, that some of the natives had already expressed their approval of the West Dock scheme. Meetings, placards, petitions and counter petitions, pamphlets in favour and those reviling the scheme poured from the presses, running the gamut of studied reasoning to downright abuse.

It is most likely that from the pamphlet war that the Hartlepool monkey drew its true genesis. An unusual bill from this period appears to be the earliest documentary reference which could be

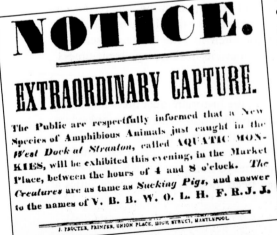

attributed to the legend. The document is a small bill by general comparison, and unusual for the period, was printed in red (Figure 1). Notable historian Robert Wood presumed that the initials printed stood for the Hartlepudlians who favoured the West Dock scheme. An even odder notice refers to that other protagonist in the area of

Figure 1. A nineteenth century advertising bill printed by J Proctor's of Hartlepool. *Author's collection*

HURRAH! HURRAH!

Victory! The show of the monkies did not take place tonight in consequence of the animals being rather unmanageable.

But tomorrow night will be seen in the Market Place a Fisherman trying on a new suit, and will at the same time read his Will stating that he may never return alive from London. That his likeness will be taken by the Stockton and Hartlepool Railway for services performed. The Performance to commence at 7 precisely no mistake.

The Public may rely that they will not be disappointed.

Figure 2. A nineteenth century advertisement relating to a fisherman. *Author's collection*

words and wits, a fisherman (Figure 2). Wood's conclusion was that the fisherman was bribed by the Stockton and West Hartlepool Railway Company into giving evidence in London in favour of the West Dock. This would explain his new suit, reference to services performed and reason for being held up to public ridicule.

The role of Hartlepool's fishing fraternity seems somewhat ambiguous. Surely they would have nothing to gain from either railway undertaking and plenty to lose with the upset caused to their practices unaltered since medieval times. One curiosity here, if taken literally, regards those 'aquatic monkies', surely no one is suggesting staid businessmen were taking to bathing together. It does however, make sense if we see it as the West Docker's scheme being an enterprise of dubious honesty and themselves as charlatans. It makes sense if we identify the 'aquatic monkies' as 'jenny hanivers', a somewhat fraudulent creation of just that era. These mermaid type creatures were popular in the nineteenth century and a number remain in private hands and public collections, indeed, the Museum of Hartlepool has a fine example on display. They are half fish, half monkey and Peter Dance, in his book *Animal Fakes and Frauds*, noted that such a mermaid had been x-rayed and 'showed a complicated arrangement of wires which supported the body but failed to support the credibility of this charming mermaid' (Figure 3).

Figure 3. A 'jenny haniver', a nineteenth century curiosity, half mermaid and half monkey. *Author's collection*

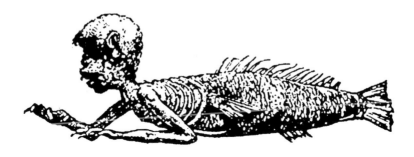

An anonymous correspondent to the *Hartlepool Mail* claimed that
a jenny haniver is a type of small skate, well known to anyone
connected with the fish quay. These can apparently be folded up,
smoked and they then take on the appearance of a small monkey. The
writer added that such was demonstrated on a stall on Lifeboat Day
in 1982. Thus there may be an unbroken tradition of jenny hanivers
or 'aquatic monkies' in Hartlepool spanning 150 years. Another
living aspect of the monkey legend.

Local Epics
The famous song associated with the monkey-hanging legend was
written by Ned Corvan (1824-1865), who as a youngster ran off with
a group of strolling players. He graduated to the music room in early
Victorian public houses and when touring, his policy was to discover
some local minor features and extend these into an epic. This he
would declaim with suitable gestures and those dramatic asides so
essential to music hall gatherings where everyone was half drunk.

Corvan wrote to Hartlepool printer John Proctor, asking him to
arrange a stage entertainment which he had devised about the life
and exploits of his mentor, the well-loved showman Billy Purvis,
whose grave is in St Hilda's churchyard on Hartlepool's Headland.
This would have been around 1855 and though it is only speculation,
we may assume that Corvan visited Hartlepool before the
performance seeking a local theme to give topicality to his act.

Back now in West Hartlepool, there was a remarkable event
concerning the new town's founder, Ralph Ward Jackson. He was
also the chief promoter of the oddly designed edifice Christ Church.
There was a falling out between Jackson and the first vicar, John Hart
Burges, and when the incumbent refused to come to heel, Jackson
had his bricklayers seal up the church doors so that the parson could
not re-enter the church. From then on, when election meetings
became heated, barrackers and hecklers would be hurling insults,
while could be heard a steady bass tone of 'Who bricked up the
church doors?' Robert Wood suggested that on the ferry on the
Headland a similar sort of slogan could be catcalled, only it would
take the form of 'Who hung the monkey?' He believed Corvan seized
on this as the basis for a comic song in 1854 or 1855 (Figure 4).

Corvan's song made its stage debut at the *Dock Hotel Music Hall*,
Southgate, Hartlepool on an unspecified date. The ballad sheet
contends it was greeted with immense applause, but it has also been
suggested the visiting entertainer was run out of town for performing
such scurrilous verses.

Figure 4. A sketch depicting part of Southgate with St Hilda's church in the background. It was at Southgate that Ned Corvan sang at the Dock Hotel Music Hall. *Author's collection*

The song, *Who Hung the Monkey?* appears in *Allan's Tynesyde Songs*, published in many editions between 1862 and 1890 and again in 1972, but under the title *The Fisherman Hung the Monkey O* (Figure 5). The latter is the authorized version, but miraculously a tattered printed copy of Corvan's original song survived the years and fortuitously passed into Robert Wood's hands. Two verses may

Figure 5. The modern version of the Monkey Song. *Author's collection*

not be deemed suitable for sensitive souls, but it is important to our heritage that Hartlepudlians are aware of the bawdy original and scholars should have access to it.

So here's the magnum opus to be sung to the tune of *The Tinker's Wedding.*

In former times when war and strife
From oe'r the channel threatened life,
When all was ready to the knife,
To watch the Frenchmen, funky O!
Chorus:-dooram'dooram'dooram, do'
&
The fishermen with courage high
Seized what they thought a real French spy.
Kill him says yan, up with him to die,
They did and they hung the Monkey, O!

•

They tried every move to make him speak,
They tortured Pug till he loud did speak,
That's French said one, says another it's Greek,
The fishermen they got drunky O!

•

He has hair all over, the wives did cry,
Oh! What un a woman with him would like;
With fish-guts then they'd bung'd up his eye,
Before they hung the Monkey, O!

•

Now some the Monkey did bewail,
For although DUMB, he had a tale (tail),
He'd sooner praps have gone to jail,
For Pug was turning funky, O!

•

The Monkey made some curious mug's
When they shaved his head and clipped his lugs,
Saying this is't way to save humbugs;
Before they hung the Monkey, O!

•

Hammer his ribs the thundering thief,
Pummet his peyte weel, man wi' your neef,
He's landed here for nought but grief,
He's Old Napoleon's uncky O!

•

To poor Pug thus, all hands behaved,
Cut off his jimmy some fools raved,
Another cries out he's never been shaved;
Before they hung the Monkey, O!

•

Then they put him on a grid iron hot,
The Monkey then quite lively got,
He grinn'd his teeth at all the lot,
And roll's his eyes quite spunky, O!

•

Then a fisherman up to Pug goes,
Let's hang him at once to end his woes,
The Monkey flew at him and bit off his nose,
Then they off to the Moor with the Monkey, O!
But let us hope that on the sea,
We'll still maintain our Soverignity,
May France and England long agree,
And never at each other get funky, O!

•

As regards poor Pug, I've had my say,
And former times have passed away,
Still you may hear to this very day,
Boy's crying who hung the Monkey, O!

What is not in doubt is that whether the Hartlepudlians liked it or not, Corvan had put them on the map.

Conclusion

A tale similar to that forever associated with Hartlepool can be found in such widespread locations as Boddam near Aberdeen, Greenock on the river Clyde, Mevagissey in south Cornwall and even in inland Derbyshire. According to writer Jonathan Raban, he found the legend in coastal Dorset and it was also told to him in Northumberland, but here the monkey was mistaken for a Spaniard. Yet I doubt, as is the case with Hartlepool expatriates, that they are greeted with, 'You're the monkey hangers!' ribaldry (Figure 6).

The legend is alive and well within Hartlepool, particularly among the sporting fraternity. The local Premier Third Division Football Club has a six foot four inch monkey mascot called H'Angus, whose antics have

Figure 6. The monkey hanging legend has been depicted on many souvenirs such as whisky flasks, tankards, club ties and as shown here, vases. *Author's collection*

Figure 7. A light-hearted re-creation of the hanging. Owen Richmond pulls the noose watched by Danny Forth. *Author's collection*

brought the town more infamy. One would have thought that amalgamation of the twin boroughs of Hartlepool and West Hartlepool in 1967 would have harmonized relationships between the rival towns, yet it did little to bring the quarrelling sides together, particularly as the 'ancient borough' lost it's council, court and separate blue buses. There are Headlanders who bewail the Heugh's plight in the local newspaper's columns, feeling they get a raw deal. As for the council, it's chief executive, Brian Dinsdale, has gone on record as saying he would prefer the monkey-hanging legend to fade away. Referring to this central aspect of the town, Dinsdale said 'Previously when Hartlepool was mentioned, people had a wry smile, but now in the region people say a lot has happened in the town and say a lot of things are nice'.

Well Brian, so is the monkey.

My own opinion, as I expressed it in my book *Who Hung the Monkey?* (Printability Publishing, 1991) is this:

> *Seriously, does it matter at the end of the day whether a monkey was really hung? There is plenty of raw data, names, places and dates. That's called history. There is also much tradition, contention and speculation. That's called myth. It is a fallacy of conventional scholarship to distinguish between these aspects with rigorous discipline and distinction. For folklore is the psychic life of a people and cannot be separated artificially from shared events. Legends may seem like lies but they always have an element of truth. Even when exaggeration and embellishments are applied, even to the extent of deliberate falsification and invention, such 'lies' of a people are not wholly gratuitous. They refer to some strata of communal reality where underlying fears, deficiencies, desires and dreams require exorcising and compensating. Their falsity makes them real; their power makes them come true. In this way a self-definition of a community is created: a collective identity occurs just when and where it is needed. It can be truth without tangibility (Figure 7).*

So, who hung the monkey, O!
    The Hartlepudlians did!

6. LOOKING BACK IN TIME: A PRINTER'S ARCHIVES

by Brian Arnison

WHEN I WAS APPRENTICED AS A BOOKBINDER in 1960 to Mr A Windross who had been in the trade for fifty years and had followed in his father's footsteps, I was following in the footsteps of my family who had worked in the printing trade for over a hundred years. Little did I know then that it would be like travelling back in a time capsule! During the next six years, as well as learning my trade I would also learn about the history of the old established Hartlepool printing works of John Proctor (Figure 1).

John was the son of Thomas Mowbray Proctor and had been apprenticed at the age of fourteen to Thomas Jennet of Stockton, who was a printer, bookbinder, bookseller and stationer. At the age of twenty-four, on 19 September 1834, John announced in the

Figure 1. Advertising signs for John Proctor. *Author's collection*

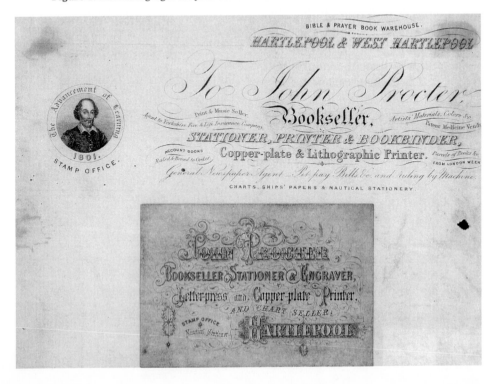

NOTICE

In consequence of the Reduction of Wages in the North, the Wages paid in these Quarries will be Reduced 2d. per Day, the Reduction to commence from Saturday, the 25th day of March, 1876.

BY ORDER,

JAS. TAIT, Manager.

Figure 2. A Proctor poster proclaiming a reduction in wages. *Author's collection*

Durham Advertiser, his intention to start his own business at Southgate in Hartlepool. He had a sign painted by Robert Brewiss on 15 October for the sum of 13s (65p). The sign advertised 'J Proctor, late assistant to Mr Jennet, Stockton Printer, Bookbinder, Bookseller & Stationer'.

Shortly after arriving in Hartlepool, John was married. He and his wife Jane had two sons, Tom and Jack who were both later educated at Gainford Academy.

The 1830s were a time of development in Hartlepool and West Hartlepool, new businesses, both large and small, were opening up, most of them requiring bookbinding and printing to be carried out in one form or another so John was in the right place at the right time to open such a business. He was one of, if not the first, printer in the area and as such was in a position to gain contracts from the new companies such as the Hartlepool Dock and Railway Company and the Gas and Water Company, at the same time the shipbuilding industry was going through a big transition within companies such as Thomas Richardson and John Spence.

From the beginning John kept all his correspondence on spike files and copies of all printed material in large guard books. A spike file was a long piece of wood with a point at one end and a metal plate at the other, the letters would be slipped onto the spike to hold them securely, a guard book was like a modern day scrap book, these were the beginnings of our present day filing system (Figure 2).

John Proctor died on 18 August 1860. A report in the *Stockton and*

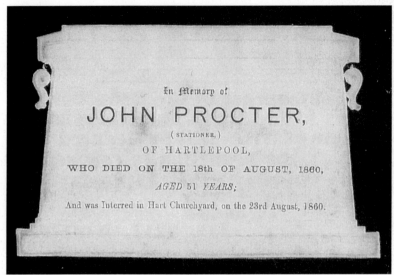

Figure 3. John Proctor's headstone in Hart graveyard. *Author's collection*

Hartlepool Mercury of 22 August had this to say of him:

> *One of the most widely known and deservedly successful tradesmen of the town, Mr Proctor served his apprenticeship with late Mr Jennet of Stockton, and had been in business for himself in Hartlepool from the early days of its commercial establishment as a coal port. His name will long be associated with the annals of the borough through his having been the publisher of the last edition of Sir Cuthbert Sharp's History. Together with an appendix from various pens; and we believe it was his intention had he lived, to have further extended the latter feature of his work. He was noted among businessmen for his promptitude, intelligence and activity; and not less for his integrity and public spirit; and his death has cast a deep gloom over the community, amongst whom his life gave an example of that rare combination the generous heart and the diligent hand. He was endeared to a numerous circle of friends by a frank and manly nature which knew no disguises, as to his nearer and dearer relations, with whom the sacred bond of an unswerving fidelity and affection has sundered he will be remembered as a model citizen. He was buried in Hart Churchyard* (Figure 3).

The printing office was later taken over by F W Mason (Figure 4) who carried on in the same tradition as John Proctor until his death in 1946 (Figure 5). When Fred Mason died the Hartlepool

Figure 4. The staff of F W Masons from left to right, back row: 1. Fergus, compositor-machine man, 2. unknown, 3. Bradley, compositor, 4.Thompson, 5. Hardcastle, billman-compositor, 6. Telfoot, litho artist, 7. Ricks, machine man, 8. unknown engineer, 9. unknown, front row: 1.Windross, bookbinder, 2. Thomson, foreman, 3. unknown engineer, 4. Bowes, compositor. *Author's collection*

Corporation asked Bertie T Ord, a printer from West Hartlepool, if he would carry on the business as they did not want the town to be without a printer and it was during this ownership in 1946 that the archives stored in the old buildings were found. Central heating was to be installed, which was to be hung from the ceiling. This meant that the plumbers had to gain access to the loft to fix large hanging brackets to support the pipes, but this they could not do because the loft was full of spike files and guard books. It was decided to dispose of all what was thought of as rubbish. On closer

Figure 5. A sporting event poster produced for Queen Victoria's Jubilee in 1887 by W Mason. *Author's collection*

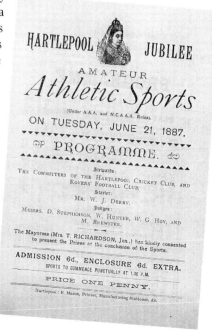

HARTLEPOOL JUBILEE
AMATEUR
Athletic Sports
(Under A.A.A. and N.C.A.A.A. Rules)
ON TUESDAY, JUNE 21, 1887.
PROGRAMME.

Stewards:
THE COMMITTEES OF THE HARTLEPOOL CRICKET CLUB, AND ROVERS' FOOTBALL CLUB.
Starter:
MR. W. J. DERRY.
Judges:
MESSRS. D. STEPHENSON, W. HUNTER, W. G. HOY, AND M. BREWSTER.

The Mayoress (Mrs. T. RICHARDSON, Jun.,) has kindly consented to present the Prizes at the conclusion of the Sports.

ADMISSION 6d., ENCLOSURE 6d. EXTRA.
SPORTS TO COMMENCE PUNCTUALLY AT 1.30 P.M.

PRICE ONE PENNY.

Hartlepool: F. Mason, Printer, Manufacturing Stationer, &c.

inspection they found that the guard books contained examples of printed material from 1834 when the printing office first opened and the spike files held all the correspondence that related to the printed material. In Bertie Ord's own words 'he found a treasure hoard of old printed material and letters'. He took one file from 1847 to the office of the local paper, *The Mail,* but they showed no interest in the material. A headmaster, Robert Wood, saw the file and he was definitely very interested! He approached Bertie Ord, and was given permission to collect the material. I met Robert in 1961 when I started my apprenticeship, a friendship and a bond formed between us as we both had similar interests. The loft space was difficult to access and as Robert was a big man and as I at the time was quite small I agreed to go into the loft and dig out the remainder of the material. Over the next few years he spent many hours sifting through the spike files and guard books, cleaning and restoring the letters and the printed material. It was estimated that there were 50,000 documents in total (Figure 6). Over the years Robert built up a wonderful archive of theatre bills and posters, he also collected a very large amount of information on the social life in the area and gave many talks and lectures, he wrote weekly articles for the *Northern Daily Mail.* Eventually he wrote a book *The History of West Hartlepool* and then a book called *Victorian Delights,* which is full of illustrations of old theatre bills and various events of the era.

The greatest printing job John Proctor will be remembered for was

Figure 6. A Proctor poster advertising a cure for all ailments. *Author's collection*

MRS. JANE COLE,

(Sister to the late JOHN PEACOCK, of Newcastle,)

Has in her possession an old Family Recipe, which perfectly cures the following Disorders, viz:—the wet and dry Scurvy, in its most inveterate state; running sores in the Legs, Arms, &c., although they be of 20 years standing; Scrofula, or King's Evil; Cancers, Scalds, or Burns, it immediately removes, without blistering, if applied soon after the accident takes place; for Scald Head or Wounds of every Description, it will be found an universal Remedy; Chilblains, or Affections from severe Frost, it removes in a short time; Swellings and Bruises taken down in 24 Hours. By damping a Linen Cloth, and applying it every morning for a fortnight, it is a never-failing remedy for Corns, also a ready Cure for the Piles, Cholera, &c.

The value of this Medicine has now found its way through the medium of Sea Captains, from Aberdeen to the Lands End of England; and she has in her possession a variety of Documents, to prove the wonderful Cures it has performed.

When applied to Green Wounds, annoint the Parts Affected with a Feather, three times a Day; but for Rheumatism or Swellings, apply the Hand by rubbing, and bind the part up with a Flannel.

Two Teaspoonfuls to be taken for Pains inwardly.

APPLY TO

Mr. Wm. COLE,

GROCER,

North Terrace, Pout's Field, Hartlepool.

the publishing of Cuthbert Sharp's *History of Hartlepool* second edition in 1851, which was printed in parts, half bound in leather. I am lucky enough to have in my possession what are probably the only originally printed copies of most of the parts.

Cuthbert Sharp was born in Hartlepool in 1771, the son of Cuthbert Sharp, a ship owner (nowadays this would be an important trade but then it was not unusual for a person to have part ownership or to own a ship). Cuthbert's mother was Susannah Crosby who came from a well-known Stockton family, her older brother was the famous Brass Crosby who became Lord Mayor of London and was imprisoned in the Tower of London by the House of Commons. He fought for rights that we take for granted today. He defied the law in 1771 and freed a printer who had been arrested in London for daring to print the debates of the House of Commons so breaching Parliamentary privilege. Such was the public outcry against Crosby being committed to the Tower because he had taken a stand for public liberties, that he was quietly released and from that time the press was allowed to publish the accounts of Parliamentary debates.

Young Cuthbert went to Dr Burney's school in Greenwich and at the age of eighteen he accepted a commission in the Essex Fencibles, which was the eighteenth century equivalent to the Home Guard. He served in Ireland at the time of the 1797 rebellion and he was present at the Battle of Arklow where the Durham Fencibles did most of the fighting. Once the fighting was over and the regiment was disbanded he attended Edinburgh University. In 1801, he visited France, but whilst there, in 1802 fighting broke out again and he was taken as a prisoner of war. Luckily he was not imprisoned at the fortress of Verdun as the others were, due to his friendship with Monsieur Regnier, President of the High Court of Justice, he was allowed to remain in Paris where he stayed for a few years. He then received permission to visit Holland, and from there returned home. The next mention of Cuthbert appears in the records at Hartlepool when on 15 April 1813 when he was appointed as one of the commissioners by the Act for improving the pier and port of Hartlepool (Figure 7) and on 2 August he was made chairman by Lieutenant John Quelch R N Clerk. He was awarded £50 for his services. In 1816 he received a knighthood from the Prince Regent.

It was in his early years when he first arrived in Hartlepool that he made a lot of friends in the literary and social scene and one particular person was Robert Surtees of Mainforth, the historian of Durham. Cuthbert carried out quite a lot of work on family trees for the Surtees Society history volumes. If you look closely at these

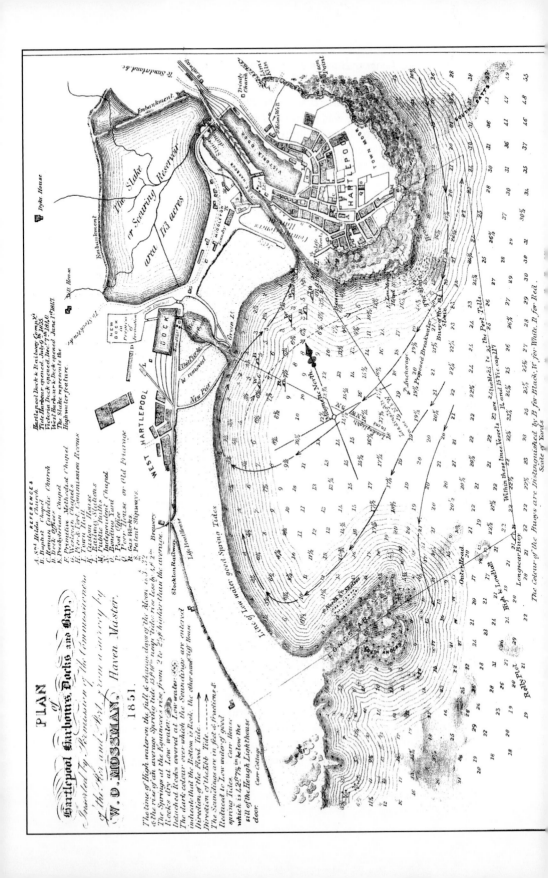

PLAN
of
Hartlepool Harbours, Docks, and Bay,

Inserted by Permission of the Commissioners

from a survey by

W. D. MOSSMAN, Haven Master.

1851.

The time of High water on the full & change days of the Moon is 3 . 22
& the rise of an average Spring tide 15 feet neap Tides rise less by 4 to 2 feet
The Springs at the Equinoxes rise from 2 to 2½ feet higher than the average.
Rocks dry at Low water :::::
Detached Rocks covered at Low water .:.:
The dark colour over which the Soundings are entered
indicates that the Bottom is Rock. the other sand Cliff House
Direction of the Flood Tide. ⟶
Direction of the Ebb Tide. ---→
The Soundings are in feet & fractions &
Reduced to Low water of good
spring Tides.   Carr house
which is 1.28¾ in below the
sill of the Heugh Lighthouse
door.   Carr Cottage

REFERENCES

A. Sᵗ Hilda Church.
B. Baptist Church.
C. Roman Catholic Church
D. Dock Offices
F. Primitive Methodist Chapel
G. Wesleyan Chapels
H. Park & Fort. Commission Rooms
I. Pier Toll
K. Custom House
L. Railway Stations
M. Public Baths
N. Independent Chapel
O. Lifeboat yard
P. Post Office
Q. Pier House or Old Priorie
R. Gas Works
S. Patent Slipways.

Hartlepool Docks & Railway Comᵖᵃⁿⁱ
Tide Harbour opened June 1ˢᵗ 1835
Victoria Dock opened Dec ᵗʰ 7ᵗʰ 1840
West Hartlepool Dock opened June 1ˢᵗ 1847
The Slake represents the
Highwater feature.

The Colour of the Buoys are Distinguished by B. for Black. W. for White. R. for Red.
Scale of Yards

books you will see the initials C S ornamented by a rose.

When Cuthbert was Mayor of Hartlepool in 1816, his first edition of the *History of Hartlepool* was published in Durham City and sold for the princely sum of one guinea (£1.1s). The book was dedicated to George Allan because Cuthbert used his vast collection of medieval manuscripts for research. Robert Surtees reviewed the book in *The Gentleman's Magazine* and wrote the following:

Nowe, by Seint Cuthberte, 'tis a worthy werke
And travaylde with rare payne and dylygens

In 1823 Cuthbert was appointed to the collectorship of the customs at Sunderland, he was there until 1845 when he was promoted to Newcastle where he died on 17 August 1849. He will long be remembered as one of the best amateur historians of his day. His most important work was his *History of the Rebellion of 1569-1841*.

Another great character of the day and a legend in the North East was Billy Purvis. Originally he earned his living as a carpenter but took every opportunity to appear on stage before the public in dramatic parts which was where he thought his talents lay. Little did he know that one day he would become one of the best-known clowns of the time. When I was working in London thirty years ago I was passing Liberty's in Argyle Street and noticed in the shop window, a three foot, hand painted wooden statue of Billy Purvis dressed as a clown, which goes to show he made it to the big city eventually. One of his parts was playing Norval in a melodrama called Douglas, where he appeared with a sword and proclaimed:

My name is Norval, on the Grampian Hills. My father feeds his flock

At these words a voice from the galley bawled out:

Ye're a great leer! Yor father an' mither sells apples an' peers in Denton Chare.

It was in 1826 he established himself as he appeared at Glasgow, Paisley, Kilmarnock and Dundee. The weather for that summer was dry, perfect conditions for travelling showmen. On his return to Hartlepool he embarked on a project to set up a theatre, which in later years became known as the Royal Victoria Theatre. His daughter boasted after his death that his was:

a proper good company', a reg'lar theatrical lot' Hamlet, Othello and aall Shakespeares plays.

The troupe wintered at Hartlepool for six months of the year and

Figure 7. Mossman's map of 1851 showing the Hartlepool docks and bay. *Author's collection*

Figure 8. Two of the theatre bills that were printed by Proctor for the travelling shows. *Author's collection*

started travelling at Easter when the weather began to improve, they would visit Shields, Blyth, Bedlington and many other places, finishing up at the October Fair at Sunderland before returning to Hartlepool once more. I remember as a lad in the 1950s delivering newspapers to the travelling showmen in the market yard and having to collect the money daily in case they moved on to a different town (Figure 8).

A contemporary of Billy Purvis in his day described him as 'Stealing the Bundle':

It was a rare treat to see Billy steal the bundle. It was never the same thing twice. The drellery was always fresh. The discovery of the bundle-the speculation as to who it belonged to-what might be its contents-whether it would be safe to open-whether it really had or had not, an owner-whether the man or the woman who laid it there had stolen it, or thrown it away because tired of carrying it-whether the owner would ever come back for it-whether, if he would be detected-whether there was, such a thing after all, such a thing as stealing-whether every appropriation of a thing was not stealing-whether one could be said to steal a bundle like that when no-one seemed to have any better claim to it-what would he do if he took and opened the bundle, and found the contents to be so and so, as tobacco, groceries, clothes, or something else-. All this monologue or soliloquy delivered in the purest Tyneside vernacular, with irresistibly comic favial and manual actions, was certain to bring down the house. And when at length he did 'lowse' the bundle, what revelations.

Billy died on 16 December 1853 at the age of sixty-nine and was buried in St Hilda's Churchyard.

I have also collected a variety of posters over the years (Figure 9-10). A letter that stands out from the collection saved by John Proctor was one from his nephew Martin Kirtley, writing from London:

Figure 9. Proctor's posters advertising the sale of the *Fleece Inn* in 1875 and a wrecked vessel in 1844, a common occurrence in the nineteenth century. *Author's collection*

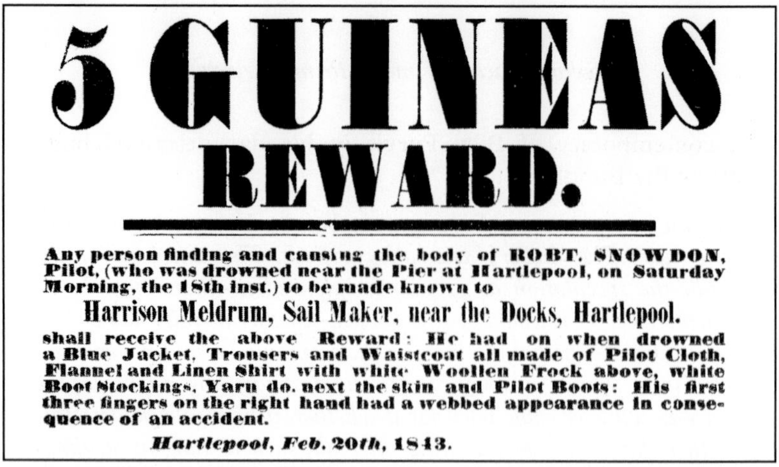

5 GUINEAS

REWARD.

Any person finding and causing the body of ROBT. SNOWDON, Pilot, (who was drowned near the Pier at Hartlepool, on Saturday Morning, the 18th inst.) to be made known to

Harrison Meldrum, Sail Maker, near the Docks, Hartlepool.

shall receive the above Reward: He had on when drowned a Blue Jacket, Trousers and Waistcoat all made of Pilot Cloth, Flannel and Linen Shirt with white Woollen Frock above, white Boot Stockings, Yarn do. next the skin and Pilot Boots: His first three fingers on the right hand had a webbed appearance in consequence of an accident.

Hartlepool, Feb. 20th, 1843.

Figure 10. A Proctor poster of 1843 advertising a reward for the finding of a body. *Author's collection*

Dear Uncle

I am just going to begin as the showman says I have often wished to see some fine men, I mean soldiers, and I am glad to say I had my wish gratified today.

I saw the Crimean Heroes enter the city. I think I shall never forget it as long as I live. In the column there were detachments of the Grenadier, Fusilier and Coldstream Guards I daresay they did not look quite so gay as when they went out, they have been too well managed for that every man without exception was as brown as a penny, their coats threadbare, muskets literally white with use, flags torn with shot, caps instead of being black were brown, but there seemed to be a lion like expression on every man's countenance. The citizens cheered but not many of the men smiled and still there seemed to be a proud and martial bearing. One man had a cat on his shoulders another had a dog which seemed proud of its situation. I was very amused at an old Turk; the man ran in front of the column, took off his cap and gave them three times three. I can assure you I felt as if I could have gone and shaken hands with every man in the regiment.

An advertisement that I thought worthy of note and quite funny was like an ad for pronto print entitled 'Chop Off the Cat's Tail'. In this age of 'rush' it is not surprising to see the methods adopted by some people to save time:

A prominent businessman in Hartlepool who values his time at so much as a second, has a Maltese cat in his office of which he is very fond. One day last week while holding the door open for the cat to go out, it struck him that half the time was lost in waiting for the tail to escape; he then got down to figures, with the following results: He opened that door at least ten times a day-to let that cat out-it took him one minute each time, and with three hundred working days in each year he found that he had been standing with that door knob in his hand for fifty hours in each working year – FIVE WHOLE WORKING DAYS!! And nothing to show for it.

He immediately ordered to cut off the cat's tail, and he now opens the door and slams it in a jiffy, without danger of hurting the cat and very little loss of time to himself.

This is only one instance; another instance of his wisdom is that:

When he requires any printing done he does not chase himself downtown, neither does he send a clerk all over creation getting estimates; experience has taught him that it is only necessary to send his orders to FW Mason's and that is the end of it: he knows perfectly well that he will turn it out promptly, and reasonably. This man is wise-time is money. Moral: Chop off the cat's tail and get your printing done at MASON'S High Street, Hartlepool, and Church Street West Hartlepool. Perhaps some of you who read this think it is time I chopped off this tale. All right! Remember one thing-when you want anything in the line of printing you can save time, bother and money, by coming to me.

FWMASONDIDITANDDELIGHTEDINIT

Written correctly - F W MASON DID IT AND DELIGHTED IN IT.

List of theatres in Hartlepool and West Hartlepool:
Theatre Royal, Northgate Hartlepool, Manager – Mr Scott.
Royal Victoria Theatre, Victoria Dock, Hartlepool, Manager – Mr Matthews.
Purvis's Theatre, Hartlepool, Manager – Mr Matthews.
Theatre Royal, West Hartlepool.
New Theatre Royal, Opposite the railway station.
West Hartlepool, Manager – Mr Maclagan.

Acknowledgments

To Maureen Anderson who planted the seed for this contribution. The late BT Ord and Robert Wood, if not for them the archives would not have been saved. Elizabeth Law of the Art Museum Events section who helped me with my research. Hartlepool Borough Council. Hartlepool Reference Library and the Hartlepool Mail. Last but not least thanks to photographer Cyril H Hull ABIPP.

7. ZEPPELIN LISTENING POSTS

by John W Perrin

The part the listening posts played in formulating the air defence of Britain and in particular the North East of England in the First World War (1914-18).

The early defence of the North East
THE URGENT CONSTRUCTION OF THE SOUND MIRRORS in various parts of Britain around 1916 was in response to the Zeppelin raids on Britain from their bases in Germany. The threat of air attack on this country was a new fear the nation had to face and together with the construction of the structures, several squadrons of aircrafts were positioned along the east coast of England in anticipation of these attacks. However, prior to these actions being implemented, the North East had suffered its first Zeppelin raid on Tyneside on 4 April 1915. Many more were to take place before the final raid on 13 March 1918, which was over Hartlepool, Middlesbrough and Redcar. Events both here in the region, in London and the Midlands forced the Government to implement a strategy of home defence.

The shooting down of Zeppelin L34 over Hartlepool Bay on the night of 27/28 November 1916, and the loss of Zeppelins in similar fashion further south demonstrated that early warning measures seen as the listening posts or acoustic sound mirrors, the positions of Home Defence Flying Corps Squadrons and better co-ordination with gunnery positions would have immediate benefits. However, as the war raged on, a new threat emerged when on 13 June 1917 twenty German Gotha Bombers attacked London without loss.

There was an immediate public outcry and the Government responded by setting up the London Air Defence Area (LADA). This brought together under co-ordinated command all the gunnery, aircraft and early warning systems, and was able to respond more successfully to further attacks, and so prove that there should be a permanent Air Defence System established throughout Britain.

During the First World War, German Zeppelin and Bomber aircraft made a total of 103 bombing raids on Britain, killing 1413 persons and injuring 3407. Though, altogether it was only a small force in numbers of Zeppelins and aircraft, they caused a

Figure 1. A frontal view showing the well preserved wing walls and the smoothness of the bowl at the Fulwell site at Sunderland. *Author's collection*

considerable disruption of civilian life, held up industrial production and retained large numbers of troops and airmen in Britain, instead of them being deployed to the battlefront in France.

The person chosen to implement LADA was a Major General FB Ashmore. He was a very experienced pilot, having obtained his flying certificate in September 1912, (No 281). Apart from expertise in artillery, he had extensive knowledge of air warfare as he had commanded the Royal Flying Corps Wing, attached to the first army in France in the autumn of 1915.

Following the end of hostilities, a conference was held at The War Office in February 1919, presided over by Winston Churchill, in his capacity of Secretary of State for War and Air. It was decided that it was essential to keep alive 'The Intricate and Specialised Art of Air Defence.' Major General Ashmore was eventually to be given the task of implementing this Home Defence Policy.

Listening posts or acoustic sound mirrors
Five sound mirrors were constructed along the North East coast at:

Fulwell, Sunderland.
Grid ref. NZ388 596
North of Sunderland on the A1018
After crossing the B1291 crossroads, with the windmill on the left, turn into a small lane, which goes up to a sport's ground. The post is situated on high ground to the left (Figures 1, 2 and 3).

Figure 2. Looking east out to sea from the site with the Fulwell Windmill to the extreme right. Note all the sites are situated on high ground. *Author's collection*

Figure 3. The plaque located on the side of the structure by the City of Sunderland authority. *Author's collection*

Figure 4. The listening post at Hartlepool was situated near to the trees by the path at the end of this housing development in Clavering Road. No trace remains. *Author's collection*

High Springwell, Hartlepool.
Grid ref. NZ 4846 3541
Clavering Road, Hartlepool. The site was on this road just to the north of the entrance to Clavering Primary School. No visible evidence remains (Figure 4).

Wheatlands Farm, Marske, Redcar.
Grid ref. NZ 6148 2295
Follow along Greenstones Road and the post is situated on the corner of Holyhead Drive. There is a lot of new housing in this locality (Figure 5).

Figure 5. This is a frontal view of the Wheatlands Farm site and is similar in size and construction to the Boulby Cliff site. *Author's collection*

DANGEROUS

STRUCTURE

Figure 6. A rear view of the Boulby Cliff site, showing how the reinforced concrete is breaking away to reveal corrugated iron shuttering beneath. The horizon is the cliff edge to the North Sea. *Author's collection*

Boulby Cliff, Easington Road, Redcar.
Grid ref. NZ 7523 1913
Situated on private land near Boulby Barn Cottage. Turn into a lane sign-posted Boulby Mine. The site is a short drive along the road on the right hand side (Figures 6 and 7).

Figure 7. A side view of the Boulby Cliff site taken from the north. This site is on private farmland. *Author's collection*

Kilnsea, Spurn Head, East Yorkshire.
Grid ref. TA 4106 1664
Four of the sites have survived in reasonable condition, but the Hartlepool post was destroyed in the 1960s when the Clavering area was developed for a new housing estate, no traces remain.

These large concrete structures were located on high ground or at locations with clear unobstructed visibility, usually on the coast. There are variations in the size and shape of these structures, but as a typical example, the Redcar post stands four metres high and measures 5.8 metres by 3.9 metres. It consists of a thick wall with an inclined face, which contains the bowl shaped reflector and has wing walls at either end. The reflector has a smooth bowl with a radius of three metres, inclined at about eleven degrees from the vertical and measures 4.6 metres across. At a glance one would assume the Kilnsea post was to an earlier standard, with no wing walls.

All the surviving posts have preservation orders placed on them owing to their historical importance, it is a great pity that the Hartlepool structure disappeared without trace.

Elsewhere in Britain, Zeppelin Posts or Acoustic Mirrors of varying shapes built of concrete were located around the Thames Estuary, on the Isle of Thanet, Kent and Selsey Bill near Chichester on the south coast. Surprisingly, one was also built at Malta. Most of those in the south survive, but little is known of the Malta post.

To operate these posts, the sound of the approaching Zeppelin engines would be reflected into a microphone located at the focal point. The steel, which would have been supporting the microphone, carried wires to the headphone of the operator or ground observer, who would be positioned in a trench nearby. By moving the microphone to find the direction of the loudest sound, the observer would be able to find the bearing of the incoming Zeppelin.

The shooting down of Zeppelin L34 over Hartlepool Bay on 27/28 1916, was probably assisted by ground observers at the locally situated posts, who were members of the Territorial Army.

The Zeppelin raids
On the night of 8 August 1916, nine Zeppelins set out to attack Northern England, however no damage was done to Teesside.

On 27 November 1916, seven airships left Germany with the intention of bombing Britain, L24, L34, L35 and L36 making for the North East, the remainder heading for the industrial targets further south. Reports of the group approaching the North East coast was received at 22.15 hours, though it was sometime later before just two Zeppelins crossed the coast, L34 and L35.

It is obvious that the listening posts or sound mirrors along the coast would have picked up the sound of the engines of the Zeppelins and early warning would have been passed to the gunnery positions and to the Air Defence

Squadrons of aircraft

Number 36 Squadron C Flight, based at Seaton Carew was on high alert and two BE 2c aircraft were airborne at 21.50 hours, following a false report of Zeppelins over Seaham Harbour. For one of the pilots, 2nd Lieutenant IV Pyott, this was the second frustration of the day, during that morning he was stranded at Howden Airfield in Yorkshire for two hours after a forced landing of a BE 2c, which developed engine trouble after it's delivery flight. Following a quick return to base, he was soon airborne again, this time on a genuine alert and at 23.30 hours, flying at 9,800 feet, he saw Zeppelin L34 below, held by the Castle Eden searchlight of North Hartlepool. He dived, firing as he dived underneath at right angles, then climbed to fly parallel with Zeppelin as it passed over the town at about seventy mph. It passed over Tunstall Ground, dropping bombs as it went, passing out to sea over St Hilda's Church. Four persons were killed and many injured by these bombs. Pyott kept the Zeppelin under observation, and as it passed out to sea he aimed several long bursts at one spot on it's port quarter, and saw his tracers entering the hull. Suddenly a small patch of flame, which he first mistook for a machine gun returning his fire, spread rapidly until the entire airship was ablaze.

Close enough to his face to be scorched, Pyott watched from his plane as the Zeppelin fell into the sea at approximately 800 yards from the Headland of Hartlepool. There were no survivors from the crew. The Zeppelin was commanded by *Kapitanleutnant* Max Dietrich, he died on his forty-sixth birthday. He and his crewmember were buried in a corner of Seaton Carew's Holy Trinity Churchyard. Later, sometime in the 1960s their remains were moved to a war cemetery in Staffordshire.

Pyott landed back at Seaton Carew in his BE 2c 2738, uninjured and the plane intact.

Ian Pyott, son of an expatriate Scot living at Port Elizabeth Cape Province, was born in South Africa and educated at George Watson's College in Edinburgh Scotland. He was clearly meticulous beyond his twenty years of age, reporting that he had fired seventy-one rounds on his main attack. He could hardly have counted so precisely at the time, so presumably based the figure on the rounds remaining unspent.

Zeppelin L35, which was ten miles north of the encounter, immediately abandoned its raid. The blazing airship was also seen by the crews in the southern group of Zeppelins 70 miles away.

For his efforts that night, Ian Pyott was awarded the Distinguished Service Order. (DSO)

West Hartlepool was again under attack on the night of 13 March 1918, when just after 21.00 hours, Second Lieutenant EC Morris of 36 Squadron, Royal Flying Corps, took off in his FE 2d aircraft with his observer Second Lieutenant RD Linford, to intercept Zeppelin L42. They sighted the raider over the town at about 17,000 feet. Morris climbed to his extreme height limit, but was still 3,000 feet below the airship. The crew fired at the airship but without results, the airship then turned out to sea. Eight people were killed and thirty-nine injured from the twenty-one bombs that were dropped during the raid.

Seaton Carew Airfield

This was situated just south of Hartlepool on land which is now Hunter House Farm industrial estate. When the Home Defence Squadrons of the Royal Flying Corps was established, C flight of 36 Squadron moved there during the spring of 1916, and operated there initially with BE 2c aircraft, but were replaced later by FE 2d aircraft. No trace of the airfield survives today.

The BE 2c aircraft

The aircraft was designed as a two-seat reconnaissance or artillery observation biplane, however it was also used as a Home Defence fighter or two-seat trainer.

Three original examples survive in museums.

At the Imperial War Museum in London.

The Musee l' Air Paris in France.

The National Aeronautical Collection in Ottowa Canada.

The FE 2b aircraft

A biplane fitted with a rearward-facing engine, with an observer positioned forward in the nose with an unobstructed field of vision, however, it was found to be more suitable as a bomber than as a home defence fighter. After the end of the war nearly all FE 2bs were believed to have been dismantled.

The Zeppelin L34

There were seventeen airships in its class. They had a compliment of seventeen crew, a range of 4,598 miles and a speed of 60 mph.

Establishing a permanent national early warning system

Following the end of hostilities in 1918, Major General Ashmore attempted to form an early warning system, this consisted of posts manned by trained observers to identify and report on the imminent arrival of hostile aircraft. It was to be 1924 before the first of the Observer Corps posts were formed in Kent on an experimental bases and it was not until January 1938 that observer posts were introduced in the North East region. The observer's status during those inter-war years was as special constables and was entirely voluntary.

Conclusion

These Zeppelin listening posts or acoustic mirrors are monuments to early attempts at early warnings to the authorities of immanent air attack. The North East region can pride itself on the contribution it played and that so many have, thankfully, survived reasonably intact. It was from their primitive warnings later overtaken by the development of radar that Britain evolved and effective air defence policy for the nation. The shooting down of Zeppelin L34 was symbolic, for it demonstrated what could be achieved with co-ordinated early warning air defence.

Sources

1. *The Air Defence of Britain 1914-1918*, Putman, 1984.
2. *The Aeroplanes of the Royal Flying Corp*, Putman, 1992.
3. *Action Stations, 4; Military Airfields of Yorkshire*, Patrick Stephens Ltd, 1981.
4. *The Zeppelin; A History of German Airships 1900-1937*, David and Charles, 2000.
5. *Air War Over Great Britain 1914-1918*, Arms and Armour Press, 1987.
6 *1929 Air Defence*, Longmans, Green and Co., 1929.
7. *English Heritage North East Region*, Tees Archaeology, Hartlepool.

8. RIVER TEES: LIFEBLOOD OF THE TEES VALLEY

by Robert Woodhouse

THE RIVER TEES IS RENOWNED for its magnificent landscapes and dramatic buildings such as the Bowes Museum and medieval fortress at Barnard Castle but it is easy to overlook the river's importance in shaping the development of the lower section of the Tees Valley. A journey from Darlington's western boundary through to the river mouth offers a series of intriguing clues to the waterways earlier importance.

The buildings of the Tees Cottage pumping station and its successor, the Broken Scar treatment works dominate the skyline on both sides of the A67 road on Darlington's western fringe. Towns in the lower Tees Valley grew considerably during the mid-nineteenth century and the demand for a reliable water supply led to the development of the site from the late 1840s. From 1849 a number of pumps were installed on the south side of the roadway to lift water from the Tees. After settlement, treatment and filtration, the water was delivered into Darlington, but as demand increased further treatment capacity was established to the north of Coniscliffe Road. In 1926 a major expansion of installations was completed, but original machinery was retained as backup. Modernization of the treatment plant brought an increase in capacity during 1955, and in 1972 another extension was added to the 13,000,000 gallon per day plant. The increasing demand for water on Teesside was met by discharging water into the Tees and its tributaries from reservoirs in Upper Teesdale.

During 1980, original buildings at Tees Cottage were threatened with demolition, but in November 1980, a charitable trust was formed to preserve buildings and equipment. Since then, members have carried out restoration work on buildings and equipment, including the three pumping systems, which were all the height of innovation in their time. The beam steam engine pumped more than 4,000,000 gallons per day before being replaced in about 1914 by a gas engine. An electric pumping system of 1926 is of equal interest and features of the pumping station are regularly opened to the public with both steam and gas engines in action.

Down the centuries, the Tees' most important role has been as a trade route with a series of shipping facilities along its banks as far upstream as the highest tidal point at Worsall Wath (above Yarm). Low Worsall was a small agricultural community until 1732 when Richard and Thomas Peirse began to develop port facilities. Construction of a stone quay and warehouses opened up an era of prosperity as merchandise from Swaledale and Teesdale, particularly wool and lead, was shipped out through Peirsburgh or Peirsport. In spite of obstacles in the river between Worsall and Yarm and problems with landowners when vessels had to be dragged around bends, local farmers and tradesmen used this tiny port facility in preference to Yarm.

As trade prospered, materials were imported to enlarge the building at the northern end of the green that became known as Worsall Hall. The 1750s were the best years for trade at Peirsport when three round-bottomed boats as well as a forty-ton sloop *Cumberland* were involved in coastal trade with Northern Europe and Scotland. Soon afterwards improvements were made to local roads and in 1764, work on Stockton's first bridge got underway, both factors were to bring an end to river trade at Low Worsall. Stones from the quay were used to build a new church on a roadside site in 1893 and during the 1920s the Tees Valley Water Board built a pumping station on the site of early port buildings.

For about 600 years – between the twelfth and eighteenth centuries – Yarm was the major port on the Tees. Sailing ships ranging from 60 to 100 tons loaded exports of flour, wool, grain, hides, salt and lead at wharves that stretched from Silver Street downstream to the site of the skinnery on Atlas Wynd. The growth of Stockton ended Yarm's days as a port and few of the granaries and warehouses are still standing but the Dutch style Yarm Hall, which dates from 1710, illustrates the links between Yarm and the Low Countries at that time. Pantile roofs are a feature of many buildings along Yarm High Street serving as a reminder that they were shipped into Yarm as ballast by vessels returning from Holland.

During troubled periods, such as the English Civil War, the Tees and its crossing points assumed strategic importance and for brief periods it marked the boundary between England and Scotland. But it was the industrial growth of the nineteenth century that saw the Tees playing a central role.

During the eighteenth and early nineteenth centuries, Stockton grew in importance as a shipbuilding centre (Figure 1) and local yards built vessels for the Royal and Merchant navies as well as a large number of colliers to serve the busy North Sea coal shipping

Figure 1. Stockton, showing building work being carried out. *Author's collection*

businesses. A number of associated trades supplied materials such as linen, cloth, sailcloth, ropes and ship firings. This expansion continued during the nineteenth century, until the late 1800s saw shipbuilding enterprises move down river to the booming development on the riverside at Middlesbrough.

The river Tees played a key role in railway history when the Stockton and Darlington Railway began coal shipments from Stockton riverside. Proprietors and coal wagons were transported from Brusselton near Shildon through Darlington and Middleton St George into Stockton where more than 100 'gentlemen' celebrated with a dinner at the Yarm house. The main players in this business

venture were a group of Darlington based Quakers led by Joseph
Pease and in 1829 they bought the Middlesbrough estate for
£30,000. Their shared intention was to develop this land as a port
facility to rival large and well-established ports like Sunderland and
even Newcastle. In 1826, Pease estimated that 10,000 tons of coal
could be exported annually from Teesside, but during the first year
after extension of the S&D Railway to Middlesbrough in 1830,
exports totalled more than 150,000 tons. By 1840, coal exports had
risen to more that one and a half million tons and improvements to
dock facilities opened the door to the town's first industry.

Middlesbrough pottery had opened on a site in Lower
Commercial Street during 1834 and in the same year, riverside
wharves were used to ship items to Gibraltar. Foreign sales
continued to play a part in the success of the town's first business
venture as the mid Victorian boom period began to take shape.

As the Tees began to play an increasingly important role in
industrial expansion, schemes were carried out to straighten the
main river channel. On 18 September 1810, Stockton's town hall was
the venue for a celebratory dinner to mark the opening of a 'cut'
between Stockton and Portrack (known as the Mandale cut) and on
10 February 1831, a further round of merry-making in Stockton
High Street marked a second operation. A channel measuring 1100
yards in length and seventy-five yards in width replaced the torturous
meander between Blue House Point and Newport.

During the following year, a Captain Hewitt surveyed the Tees for
the Admiralty and included, among a number of suggestions made at
that time, was a practical scheme aimed at improving the mouth of
the Tees by constructing a breakwater. Completion of breakwaters –
or Gares – at Tees mouth did not take place until the second half of
the nineteenth century. South Gare is some two and a half miles in
length and construction lasted from 1863 to 1888 at a total cost of
£219,393. Some 7,000,000 tons of slag from nearby blast furnaces
was moved by rail to form the basis of the concrete covered structure.
Features included on South Gare are; Paddy's Hole – a man made
harbour – lifeboat station, pilot's station and 'tacky shades' which
measure dust in the atmosphere. North Gare is a half-mile long and
was constructed between 1882 and 1891 at a cost of £65,531.

From 1852, improvements to the river were in the hands of the
Tees Conservancy Commissioners and during the second half of the
nineteenth century they greatly altered the physical character of the
Tees. Some £200,000 was spent on dredging the main channel as
well as localized schemes in the Stockton area, and some £590 was

Figure 2. Tugs moored at Cargo Fleet. *Author's collection*

spent on the 'removal of obstructions' between Stockton bridge and Yarm. By 1900, the Commissioners owned seven tug boats (Figure 2) and a steam barge (at a total cost of over £31,000) and in 1875 they had taken a major decision to open a growing dock at South Bank (which opened for public use in November 1876).

An important advantage offered by the Tees was its low tidal range and this was a factor that affected some niney-eight acres of land downstream from Newport bridge and within a great curve of the river. Lines of timber wharves spread along the riverbank when industrialists built blast furnaces, furnaces and rolling mills on this sector of low-lying land. Dorman Long took several of these businesses over in later years and the longest operating blast furnace plant was the Ayresome Ironworks, which continued in use from 1872 to 1965.

Before this massive industrial expansion, local folk had gathered

Figure 3. The Furness Shipyard at Haverton Hill. *Author's collection*

mussels along tidal flats in the Newport area and the townspeople of
Yarm had drawn off drinking water from the Tees but by the 1920s
pollution levels were rising rapidly.

Industrial developments on both banks continued apace. A rail
link to Port Clarence allowed coal shipments from the north bank to
begin in 1834 – in direct competition with the S&D line across the
river. Iron and glass works were opened on adjacent land and the
opening of the Losh Bell and Company ironworks in 1853 brought a
major influx of workers and their families. A new community grew up
in the shadow of the extensive works and Bell Brothers (who took over
the Losh Bell Company) provided a school for local children, followed
by employment in their foundries for boys of school-leaving age.

The banks of the Tees were also the base for a tradition of
shipbuilding and in 1917; low-lying land at Haverton Hill was
reclaimed to accommodate the Furness Shipyard (Figure 3). Women,

ex-servicemen and Irish navvies carried out much of the construction work. A steamer of 10,000 tons was the first vessel to be launched at the yard in 1919.

Until the twentieth century, Stockton's Victoria bridge (Figure 4) was the lowest crossing point on the Tees but as the volume of trade and commerce increased, the lower section of the river gained two bridges of unusual and innovative design. Both structures had to allow river traffic to pass upstream to Stockton and each one adopted a different approach. Prince Arthur of Connaught opened the Transporter bridge on 17 December 1911 and the bridge had a suspended carriage running across the central span, while Newport bridge had a massive central lifting span. Opened by HRH the Duke of York on 28 February 1934, it had a 120-foot clearance between the high-water mark and central span when it was in the raised position.

Downstream from Middlesbrough, the southern bank of the Tees was developed with shipping facilities and industrial premises. In some places, sectors of land were opened up to provide additional dock areas. In 1840, work got underway on Middlesbrough dock and water was first channelled into the new facility on 19 March 1842. The original water area of nine acres was extended in 1869, 1885 and 1895, to give a total of over twenty-five acres with ten berths. Access from the main river course was through an entrance channel, which was crossed by a swing bridge. Exploitation of iron-ore deposits in the Cleveland Hills after 1850 and construction of the rail link between Middlesbrough and Redcar, which opened on 4 June 1846, brought rapid industrialisation along the final stretch of the southern bank.

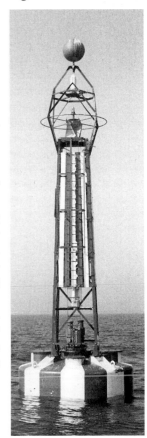

In 1963, another area of land was carved out of the south side. It has five cargo berths along two quays with four single storey transit sheds providing about 30,000 square metres of storage space. Later additions include the Steel Export Terminal, which became operational in November 1976, and a roll-on roll-off berth at the inland end of the dock opened in 1973.

Until dredging operations created a main channel for sea-going vessels, the mouth of the river consisted of extensive mudflats and shifting sands (Figure 5). By 1900 more than half of Tees mouth's

Figure 5. Fairway buoy, situated at the estuary in Tees Bay. *Author's collection*

Figure 4. Stockton's Victoria bridge. *Author's collection*

2,400 hectares of inter-tidal mudflats had been reclaimed by industrial use and during the 1960s and 1970s much of the remaining land was also developed, leaving little more than 160 hectares of mudflats. The importance of this estuarial land led to its designation as a Grade 1 Site of Special Scientific Interest, with forty-six species of wading birds recorded at the location, which represents the only feeding area for transient and migratory birds on England's east coast between the Humber Estuary and Fenham Flatts.

On the north bank, Bitmac Limited occupies land downstream from the Transporter bridge and storage tanks cover the adjacent land. Closer to the river mouth, the Seal Sands site provides a base for Phillips Petroleum Company's operations in the North Sea. Oil and gas liquids from the Ekcofisk field are pumped through a 220-mile pipeline to the terminal at Seal Sands where they are separated. Crude oil is loaded onto tankers at adjacent deepwater berths for shipment to refineries in Western Europe and elsewhere. Some crude oil is also piped to the nearby Philips Imperial Petroleum Refinery at North Tees. Natural liquid gases are further separated into methane, ethane, propane and butane.

Greatham Creek feeds into the northern side of the wide estuary and the most prominent landmark on this low-lying expanse of former mudflats is Hartlepool Power Station, (Figure 6) which first supplied electricity to the grid in 1972, some four years after construction work began.

The jutting steelwork of Redcar Ore Terminal demonstrates the lower section of the southern bank. Opened in 1973 at a cost of £23,000,000, it was a joint venture between British Steel and Tees and Hartlepool Port Authority. Three giant inloaders can work on ships of up to 150,000 dead weight tonnage with a handling capacity of around 10,000,000 tonnes of coal and coke annually. Raw materials are stacked and blended before being fed into production plants by conveyor systems and then charged to the nearby Redcar furnace.

The closing decades of the twentieth century saw dramatic changes along the tidal section of the Tees. The last vessel left Stockton's Corporation Quay in August 1967 and the sector of land that was covered by a railway line, warehousing and riverside taverns has been redeveloped with a dual carriageway and riverside footpath. River based trade and industry continued to more downstream and during summer, 1989, a Bill passed through Parliament to allow bolting down of Newport bridge in order to save maintenance and replacement costs

Industry continued to give way to leisure on the banks of the Tees above Middlesbrough. Industries on the ironmasters' site declined during the post-war years and during the 1970s, most of the area was reclaimed as grassland with a pleasant riverside walkway. A former slagheap was landscaped as a recreation area and the twelve-acre Tressaurus Park was officially opened by the mayor of Middlesbrough, counsellor Charles Godfrey on 17 June 1982. A self-guided walk 'the Ironmaster Trail' was compiled to highlight former industrial locations.

Movement of shipping and trade towards the mouth of the river continued with the closure of Middlesbrough Dock at the end of July 1980. Several of the dock's newer cranes were transferred to Tees

Figure 6. Hartlepool Nuclear Power Station. *Author's collection*

Figure 7. Ships moored at Tees Dock. *Author's collection*

Dock, (Figure 7) 17 others, weighing between 54 and 110 tonnes were cut up for scrap.

Development of the long-distance footpath 'Teesdale Way' focused attention on natural beauty along the river banks, plant and animal life has returned to areas such as the Portrack Marshes where a wildlife reserve has provided a habitat for a wide range of insects and birds.

The most significant change in the river's outlook came with construction of the Tees Barrage. Officially opened by HRH the Duke of Edinburgh in July 1995, at a cost of £50,000,000, the impressive structure created a ten-mile stretch of clean water from

Portrack, below Stockton to Worsall. Facilities at the Barrage include a white water course for rafts and canoes, while neighbouring sectors of land have seen removal of industrial eyesores and ongoing redevelopment schemes. The former Head Wrightson site at Thornaby (Figure 8) has seen construction of housing and business premises as well as buildings of the university campus and proposals have been put forward for more office accommodation and apartment buildings on the north bank, downstream from Stockton.

The Tees has become an asset to the towns of the lower river valley and its sporting status was recognised by the hosting of the world course canoeing championships in August 2001. Another major facility, the River Tees Water Sports Centre, was opened at Portrack on 20 November 2001 by the Sport's Minister, Richard Caborn. A whole range of people now enjoy a river setting that is far removed from the polluted industrialised waterway of the nineteenth and twentieth centuries.

Figure 8. The crowds are out to watch the launch of a ship at Thornaby. *Author's collection*

9. MONKS, MONEY AND MIDDLESBROUGH

by Geoff S Braddy

ONE OF THE GREAT PUZZLES of Middlesbrough's early history is why did Robert de Brus decide to establish a Benedictine priory there? Nothing survives of Middlesbrough Priory apart from a few sketches of its ruins drawn in the seventeenth, eighteenth and nineteenth centuries (Figure 1) and a few carved stones, which are preserved in the local museum (Figures 2 and 3). However, we know that the priory stood just a few yards north of the old town hall from 1119 until the dissolution of the monasteries, and that it survived as a ruin until the eighteenth century. The question is, why did Robert de Brus decide to found this priory on behalf of the Benedictines. There were several orders of monks in medieval England: Cistercians, Augustinians, Carthusians, Benedictines and so on, and most Norman barons had their own favourite order. In the case of Robert de Brus, the Augustinian canons must have found particular favour, for he was exceptionally generous to them. His greatest foundation was Guisborough Priory, an Augustinian monastery which he endowed so liberally that it became the fourth richest religious house in Yorkshire. At Middlesbrough he created a much smaller monastery, not for his beloved Augustinians, but for the Benedictines, the Black Monks.

> *Robert de Brus to all the faithful of the Holy Church, greetings. Know that I and Agnes my wife and our son Adam de Brus for the good of our souls and of the soul of our Lord Henry, King of England, have given and concede and confirmed to the church and the brothers of St Peter and St Hilda of Whitby the church of St Hilda the Abbess at Middlesbrough, with everything that belongs to that church and two carucates and two bovates of land in Newham in perpetual alms, on the understanding that there will be certain monks in the said church at Middlesbrough who shall serve God and St Hilda of Whitby, for whom the stipends of the said church will be more than sufficient for them to live well enough, and that the mother Church of Whitby shall always have the profits.*[1]

This foundation charter makes it clear that Middlesbrough Priory was not to be connected with Guisborough in any way, but was to

Figure 1. A sketch showing part of the ruins of Middlesbrough Priory. *The Church of England Magazine, 1846*

Figure 2. A late medieval sculpted stone head from Middlesbrough Priory. *Courtesy of Dorman Long Museum, Middlesbrough Museums and Galleries*

Figure 3. Fourteenth century stone mouldings from Middlesbrough Priory. *Courtesy of Dorman Long Museum, Middlesbrough Museums and Galleries*

Figure 4. A sketch showing the magnificence of Whitby Abbey. *Courtesy of ICI Archives at Synetix Chilton Site*

belong to the Benedictines of Whitby Abbey (Figure 4). It was not unusual for a baron such as Robert de Brus to create religious foundations for two different orders. For instance, Walter L'Espec of Helmsley who founded no less than four monastic houses granted two to the Cistercians (including Rievaulx Abbey) and two to the Augustinians (including Kirkham Priory). But why did de Brus create one large independent monastery at Guisborough and a much smaller one at Middlesbrough which was not independent, but which was to be controlled from Whitby by a different order of monks?

We may never discover the answer but there is a theory which, although only guesswork, does seem to fit the facts. The theory is that while Guisborough Priory was de Brus's own idea, Middlesbrough Priory was suggested to him by someone acting on behalf of Whitby Abbey, perhaps even the abbott himself. A site near the river Tees would have been a lucrative one. During the twelfth century several Yorkshire monasteries acquired lands beside the river Tees. Byland, Rievaulx and Guisborough were amongst them but Whitby appears to have been the first. In those days the Tees was a renowned salmon river. Indeed one local man was to grant a fishery on the Tees to Guisborough Priory specifically so that the canons could eat salmon on thirteen holy days each year.[2] Fisheries on the Tees could prove profitable as well as supplying the monks with an alternative to red meat. Monastic converts were keen to have lands and fisheries along such an excellent river. Perhaps someone convinced de Brus that it would be a worthwhile gesture to grant his Middlebrough property to the monks of Whitby Abbey with a view to them fishing there, whereupon he took the further step of insisting that a cell of monks should be maintained there. We might speculate that he was seeking to atone for wrongdoings in his younger days.

Of course, to the medieval mind, a monastery was something which should last forever, so it was necessary to adopt a method of providing funds for everyday expenses, which would never run out. The solution was that monasteries were endowed with extensive estates. Rents, produce or other profits from these estates could sustain a monastery indefinitely. De Brus granted the new priory a carucate of land at Middlesbrough and two and a quarter carucates at Newham. A carucate was not a fixed measurement such as we would be familiar with today, but it is generally reckoned to have amounted to about 120 acres. This means that the Middlesbrough monks received almost 400 acres from de Brus. Men of lesser rank then came forward, or were persuaded, to offer smaller grants of land; often only three or four acres, occasionally ten or fifteen. In some cases the extent of the grant is not specified in the charters, so it is not possible to give an accurate total, but these smaller grants certainly amounted to more that 150 acres and possibly to more than 200. The Latin transcripts of these transactions have been published by the Surtees Society,[3] while English summaries of them can be found in Kirby's Ancient Middlesbrough.[4] Only a few of the charters carry the date when they were written, but approximate dates can be worked out from the names of witnesses attached to each grant. A few early ones were apparently written soon after Middlesbrough

Priory was founded, but most seem to date from the second half of the twelfth century and the first half of the thirteenth century. In 1279 Edward I issued the Statute of Mortmain which was meant to give his government some issue of control over grants of land to monasteries. It did not prohibit such grants; it merely insisted that lords had to pay for a license to sign away their property. However, by that date, most of the lands which would have been attracted to the monks of Middlesbrough had already been granted to them, if not to Guisborough, Byland or some other religious house. In certain cases, the land was needed by its owner. In addition it was becoming the fashion for wealthy people to found chantry chapels rather than giving lands to monasteries, so the grants to Middlesbrough Priory slowly dried up.

To examine the site of the priory the modern visitor needs to go to North Street, just off the old market place, not far from the Transporter Bridge. Nothing remains now, but an eighteenth century sketch of the ruins reveals that the priory church had stout round columns and broad round arches, rather like a scaled down version of Durham Cathedral.[5] Close at hand were buildings where the monks lived, with kitchens, storerooms, a refectory, a dormitory and possibly a small cloister where they could study. The site was on the side of a low hill from which the monks would have been able to look across several hundred acres of farmland which belonged to them. In the far distance they might even have been able to glimpse their Newham estate. This lay two-and-a half miles to the south where now you will find Newburn Bridge Primary School and Sandy Flatts playing field.

The people who had been farming the land when it was handed over to the Benedictines were also handed over, almost as if they were chattels to be disposed of. Now they owed their services to Middlesbrough Priory and the Abbott of Whitby.

Each bondman in Middlesbrough gives for his bovate ten shillings, and one goose and two hens. He makes hay for one day at haytime and leads one cartload of turf or wood wheresoever the Abbott buys it, or makes recompense at the Abbott's pleasure. He takes the Abbott's food where the Abbott is staying, and if a monk stays there for eight days or more, he takes their clothes to Whitby if it is necessary. He thatches the mill; he gives geld, and he pays multure to the thirteenth measure.

The cottar of Middlesbrough gives for his cottar's tenure of one-and-a-half acres twelve pence and eight men in autumn; and twice

*shall be at the Abbott's breakfast. He gives four hens and forty eggs
and helps with leading and escorting just as the bondmen do; in
addition he carts turf and corn and gives a goose.*[6]

The bondmen were not too badly off. Each of them had a bovate of
land (fifteen acres) where he could grow crops for his family, and he
was entitled to graze his animals on the common. The bondmen's
rent of ten shillings a year was roughly equivalent to a month's wages
for a working man, but we are not told how much 'geld' they had to
pay. Bondmen were not allowed to take their corn to be ground
anywhere but the Abbott's mill, and there they had to pay 'multure'
which meant that the Abbott kept one measure of their grain out of
every thirteen measures which were ground. Bondmen had to do a
certain amount of fetching and carrying and a day's hay making each
year. When the mill roof needed thatching, they had to do it. This
work was unpaid, although food and drink were provided during the
working day.

The cottars were the poorest villagers with only one-and-a half
acres of land at a rent of one shilling a year. Like the bondmen, the
cottars had to work for the priory without pay for so many days each
year. Each cottar and his family had to do the work of eight men in
the autumn, so if there were only four in the family, they would each
have to work twice as many days. They also had to find time for
fetching and carrying for the monks. Every bondman and cottar had
to provide a goose each year, along with numbers of hens and eggs,
so the priory was always well stocked with poultry.

Judging by the earliest known map of Middlesbrough, these
families of bondmen and cottars lived in two rows of cottages on
either side of a road, which the monks called Kirkgate.[7] We know this
road as South Street and its continuations, Sussex Street and
Linthorpe Road. It stretched away southwards before taking a sharp
turn westward to the villages of Linthorpe and Ayresome. The monks
of Whitby had a bovate in Linthorpe, as did the monks of Byland and
the canons of Guisborough. However, at Ayresome the canons were
quickest off the mark when it came to acquiring property. William
Ingleram and his son John granted a carucate there to Guisborough
Priory.[8] Several smaller grants were made to Guisborough by other
benefactors, and since the Inglerams wanted to keep four carucates
there for themselves, there was little opportunity for the Whitby
monks to acquire more than a few acres around Ayresome.

The urban sprawl of modern Middlesbrough and the nineteenth
diversions of the river Tees have tended to obscure the medieval

attractions of Linthorpe and Ayresome. The Tees was considerably wider in the twelfth century than it is now, and swung round in a great loop which brought it close to Linthorpe and Ayresome. As with Middlesbrough, these villages were well placed for fisheries. The Ingleram charter for Ayresome specified that the site was useful for making fisheries, while a charter of William de Tameton granting a bovate in Linthorpe likewise mentioned a fishery. Byland Abbey also had a fishery nearby, granted by William de Acclum.[9]

As well as a lucrative fishery in the Tees, Guisborough Priory also had Ayrsome Grange. This farm is dateable through documentary evidence to the thirteenth century[10] but may have been established earlier. The canons farmed the grange as a single block of over 100 acres, stretching from Acklam Lane in the west to Kirkgate (Linthorpe Road) in the east. After the dissolution of the monasteries by Henry VIII this block of land remained in separate ownership from the rest of the district, consequently it has left its imprint on the street plan of modern Middlesbrough. While most of the town was laid out in a grid of parallel lines, modern street maps show that Gresham Road is not parallel to Ayresome Street and bends where it meets Glebe Road, while Carlow Street and the streets to the east of it are out of alignment with the other streets in that part of the town. This is all due to the shape of the canons' grange at Ayresome six or seven centuries ago.

A rent roll of Guisborough Priory from around 1300 indicates that the canons had tenants in Middlesbrough and Linthorpe as well as Ayresome. Most of the inhabitants recorded there seem to have been at the same level as the cottars of Middlesbrough Priory since they mostly paid rents of a shilling or less, had to work six or twelve boon days a year and had to provide two or four hens and 20 or 40 eggs per annum. The canons had just one or two bovate holders in each village.[11]

As well as granting lands, bondmen and fisheries to religious houses, Norman barons also granted churches. These were seized upon eagerly by the convents because they would then be entitled to receive tithes. The church of St Hilda at Middlesbrough was granted to Whitby Abbey, while the church of St Mary at Acklam was granted to Guisborough Priory by Alvered de Acclum.[12] In those days St Mary's was a chapel dependant on the mother church at Stainton, which itself was granted to Guisborough, this time by Robert de Brus. The haphazard allocation of lands, churches and rights to tithes between the Benedictines and the Augustinians was a recipe for discord and disagreements. A dispute arose between

Guisborough Priory and Whitby Abbey over the ownership of tithes.[13] The monks of Whitby had been in the habit of collecting tithes from twelve carucates of land in Middlesbrough, Ayresome and Acklam, when the canons of Guisborough contested their right to do so. They claimed these tithes for themselves. In about 1133 the dispute was settled in the presence of Robert de Brus and his two sons. Abbot Nicholas of Whitby and Prior William of Guisborough were also present when it was decided to divide the tithes equally between the two houses. Whitby was to have tithes from six of the carucates, which mostly lay in Middlesbrough and Ayresome; Guisborough was to have the tithes from the other six, most of which lay in Acklam. One of these six however lay in Ayresome and the boundary between this carucate and one owing tithes to Whitby was rather convoluted. It wound its way between some of the housing plots of Linthorpe village. One effect of this was that, for centuries some Linthorpe people were baptised, married and buried in Middlesbrough, while their neighbours worshipped in Acklam. The church of St Hilda in Middlesbrough was made a mother church, with Linthorpe village lying half in Middlesbrough parish and half in Acklam parish.

Let us now move on to the middle decades of the thirteenth century and beyond. A great deal of expensive building work was undertaken at this time, both at Whitby and Guisborough. A glance at the ruins of Whitby Abbey will be enough to convince the modern visitor that it must have once been a grand and imposing structure. Most of what you see today however is not the abbey as Robert de Brus would have known it. The present remains date from the extensive rebuilding which was undertaken at the time of Abbot Roger de Scarborough (1223-45). Roger began his career as a monk at Middlesbrough Priory and proved to be very successful at raising money for building work at Whitby. While Abbot Roger was busy re-modelling Whitby Abbey, the canons of Guisborough were worshipping in a church which would be quite unrecognizable to us today. It was totally destroyed by fire in 1289, and it was not until the early fourteenth century that the canons were able to build the splendid priory which we see today.

These massive operations at Whitby and Guisborough demonstrate that enthusiasm for religious houses was still strong in the community at large in the thirteenth and early fourteenth centuries. Nonetheless the generosity of benefactors and the various means of raising money which the monasteries devised, had their limits and before the fourteenth century was very old, Whitby Abbey and Guisborough Priory found themselves falling into debt. At Whitby the dramatic changes in fortune is highlighted in the registers of the Archbishops of York. Archbishop William Wickwane could find nothing amiss when he inspected the abbey in the 1280s, whereas Archbishop William Melton was so concerned about the state of the abbey's affairs in 1320 that he ordered a full investigation.[14]

What could have reduced a once great institution such as Whitby Abbey to debt and disorder? Perhaps the rebuilding costs had exceeded expectations; perhaps the Scottish raids following Bruce's victory in Bannockburn in 1314 had devastated the abbey's granges, or perhaps crop failures and epidemics amongst the abbey's flocks of sheep had hit hard. During the first half of the fourteenth century the monks tried various ways of relieving their debts. They sought donations, they sold off some of their assets and they tried to acquire new assets to help offset future difficulties. The records do not disclose what measure of success they had, if any, but detailed records have survived from a slightly later period, the 1360s and 1370s.[15] These documents reveal a convent torn by dissension and distrust. Middlesbrough Priory turns out to have been a hotbed for stirring up trouble and plotting against the Abbot at Whitby. The monks were divided into two opposing camps, one led by the Abbot, William de Burton, the other by the Prior of Middlesbrough Thomas de Haukesgarth. This Thomas, whose surname indicates that he came from Hawsker, was theoretically in charge of Middlesbrough Priory, but since the Priory was a 'daughter' of the 'mother' house of Whitby, he was supposed to be obedient to the Abbot. However, Thomas was far from obedient. He refused to return to Whitby when the Abbot summoned him, and he was in the habit of leaving the priory at Middlesbrough without the Abbot's permission. The Abbot claimed that when challenged, Thomas had replied that he would leave the priory whenever he pleased. We know about this quarrel from the visitation records of Whitby Abbey. Benedictine abbeys were inspected every three years and the first signs of trouble were noted during the visitation of June 1366. The situation was so bad that a second visitation was ordered in October. In an attempt to keep the situation calm, the Archbishop of York had sent the recalcitrant Prior of Middlesbrough to Selby Abbey, but presumable he was recalled to give evidence along with his fellow monks.

Medieval abbots were supposed to rule in consultation with all the brethren, meeting in chapter. Abbot William de Burton however seems to have ruled through a small clique of confidants who were often in the Abbot's chamber. This group included William de Ayton the bursar, Reginald de Esyngton the sacrist, Stephen de Ormesby the cellerar, John de Holm and Robert de Gisburn who was a close colleague of the Abbot even though he did not apparently hold any office. Other regular visitors to the Abbot's quarters were Robert Edward the chamberlain, Alan de Ake (a kinsman of the Abbot) and two wealthy local men, Thomas de Mauley and Richard de Roucliff. Ranged against the Abbot was a larger group of monks led by Thomas de Haukesgarth. They included Matthew Dawney (the Prior of Whitby) John de Alverton and Peter de Hertilpool (two Middlesbrough monks) and John de Richemund, John de Levington and John de Marton (three monks who may also have been at Middlesbrough). Three ordinary chapter monks at Whitby named William de Ormesby, Robert de Boynton and Walter Bampton also sided with this group, as did Alexander de Lythe the Abbot's steward.

Amidst all the accusations and counter-accusations it is difficult to determine what was at the root of the trouble. Perhaps it was the result of a clash of personalities between Thomas de Haukesgarth, Peter de Hertilpool and William de Burton. Thomas and Peter were former bursars of Whitby. Perhaps they resented being moved from this office and sent to Middlesbrough, away from the centre of affairs. Peter was not one to respect authority, if we accept the allegation that he tried to bring about the fall of the previous abbot, engineering a campaign which was said to have led to that abbot's death. Perhaps the root cause was the improper behaviour of several of the monks. Some were said to be adulterers. The Prior of Middlesbrough was said to have fathered sons by three different women. The Abbot himself was said to avoid matins, preferring to stay up in his room until the middle of the night 'in shameful feasting and drinking'. It was claimed that he had favourites whose sins went unpunished. A third possibility is that the root cause was William de Burton's frequent use of high-risk tactics to combat the Abbey's debts. He had been warned against such things by the church authorities who were alarmed by the risks he was taking, as no doubt were many of his brethren. What were these tactics? Firstly he sold corrodies. A corrody was an agreement to provide board and lodging within the precinct of the monastery. The corrodian paid a lump sum, and was given lodgings for the rest of his life, with no further payments to be made. If he died soon, the monastery profited from the deal, but if he lived on for many years it could prove expensive for the monks. Secondly, the Abbot leased some of the Abbey's wool. Instead of paying for one year's wool as usual, a merchant would be asked to pay a larger sum and the monastery would provide him with wool for the next three years at no extra charge. This was fine in the first year, but it meant that no income could be generated from wool sales in the succeeding two years. A third tactic was to allow an intermediary to collect some of the tithes, rents and other dues which the Abbey was entitled to receive. Again, a lump sum would be paid at the start of the agreement and nothing more for the remainder of the term. For instance, the Abbot sold three year's tithes from Nunthorpe for fourteen marks and seven years altarage from Great Ayton for £30. These tactics provided ready money, but depleted regular sources of income. Abbot William also sold a considerable number of sheep, which meant that wool sales could not be maintained at previous levels.

We can get a little closer to the root cause of the dispute by examining the complaints which the Middlesbrough monks made against Abbot William de Burton. There were a variety of accusations against the Abbot, but the emphasis lay with two aspects in particular: his financial mismanagement and his autocratic tendencies, supported by his inner circle of friends and favourites. It was claimed that the rents and revenues of the abbey had fallen from £540 per annum to £420 per annum during his time in office. Furthermore, it was claimed that although the convent had managed to get by with £420 per annum, the Abbot was still trying every means possible to raise ready money and that he was diverting some of the funds into his own treasury. He demanded a personal pension of one mark per annum (about a fifth of a parish priest's annual income) from Middlesbrough Priory and having insisted that the priory should provide a certain amount of corn for the corrodies he had sold, he proceeded to seize three times as much. The monks at Middlesbrough claimed that their priory was disfigured and that some of its buildings were ruinous because the Abbot left them without the means of paying for repairs. On the question of the Abbot's style of administration and his inner circle, the Middlesbrough monks were particularly vociferous. They attacked the morals of some of the Abbot's closest advisors. One had been convicted of adultery under the previous abbot, yet William de Burton allowed him to take his place at the high altar at Christmas and Easter. Another was said to have fraudulently withdrawn 40 marks from the kitcheners funds. A third was believed to have a considerable amount of money in his possession in contravention of his vows. A fourth was accused of keeping sacks of merchandise in the church. When the Abbot declared that he always consulted the full convent over important decisions, the Middlesbrough monks replied that he ruled the monastery by threats of excommunication against any monk who dared to oppose him at chapter. He carried out his threat on one occasion by excommunicating the Prior of Middlesbrough.

The Abbot's inner circle included men who were not in holy orders. The most notorious of these was Thomas de Mauley, who was retained by William de Burton for five marks per annum (equivalent to a parish priest's annual income) and to whom the Abbot sometimes granted favours. De Mauley reportedly threatened the friends of Prior Thomas that he would seize and imprison them if they made trouble for Abbot William. The culmination of this state of affairs came when the Prior of Middlesbrough and his 'accomplices' were said to have entered the Abbot's quarters in Whitby at night armed with 'swords, staves and other arms'. During the subsequent investigation the Middlesbrough party made a counter claim that they had found armed men standing in the cloister when they arrived for the morning's chapter meeting. They took this to be a veiled threat. If armed men were indeed stationed near the chapter house, it is likely that they were sent by Thomas de Mauley. The Prior of Middlesbrough excused some of his actions in terms of his fear of de Mauley.

Certain monks (not named in the record) appeared before the King and his council to accuse Abbot William of wasting the Abbey's resources. As a result, the King commissioned Henry Percy, William de Aton and the sheriff of York to investigate the charges. They were instructed

> to survey the state of the abbey, call before them the abbot and the monks, ministers and servants of the abbey, examine them upon the state of the abbey, the bearing of the abbot and the monks…and make inquisition touching the premises by the oath of the ministers and servants of the abbey and of the men of Whitby strand and the neighbouring parts.[16]

It was a rare intrusion by the royal government into the monastic world, a world which was already strictly regulated by its own internal system of inspection and discipline. We do not know the result of this investigation, but we do know that at some time between then and May 1371 the Abbot's enemies contrived to have him imprisoned in York Castle. William de Burton was not a man to take this lying down, and after his release he wasted little time in appealing to the King for assistance in having the Prior of

Middlesbrough brought before him for chastisement. Two of the four men who were commissioned by the King to arrest Prior Thomas were Thomas de Mauley and Richard de Roucliff, who were both in the pay of Abbot William.[17] The problems between Whitby and Middlesbrough came to an end in 1374 when William de Burton died.

Given the limitations of the evidence it is difficult to decide who was the guilty party in this long running quarrel. One problem is that the investigation relied heavily on a process called 'canonical purgation'. A monk could 'prove' his innocence through the testimony of his fellow monks. If you accept that a medieval monk would not perjure himself under oath, then we must conclude that the guilt lay more on the Abbot's side. His closest associates were not able to find brothers who would swear to their innocence. Robert de Gisburn was sent to St Mary's Abbey, York, to be punished; John de Holm was sent to Selby, Stephen de Ormesby was to be publicly disciplined in chapter for several days each month. On the other hand the Middlesbrough monks found all the witnesses they needed to testify on their behalf. In the case of Thomas de Haukesgarth himself, he admitted some of the charges, but excused himself through his fear of Thomas de Mauley's men. Several of the charges against him were placed in suspension pending further investigations, unfortunately the results are not known. In the case of William de Burton, his answers to the charges were either straight denials or rather legalistic excuses. He repeatedly insisted that decisions had been taken with the consent of the convent, but they in turn maintained that their consent was obtained under duress. Neither Thomas nor William was removed from office. Indeed, Thomas was later deemed an appropriate person to conduct the visitation of another monastery, and he remained Prior of Middlesbrough for many more years. For the next century and a half, the history of Middlesbrough Priory is rather shadowy. Very little written evidence has survived, but such as there is suggests troubles were never far away. On one occasion, the King demanded sureties of £200 to prevent Sir Robert Conyers from doing or procuring any harm to the Prior of Middlesbrough or his brethren.[18] On another occasion, Sir Thomas Boynton challenged the title of Whitby Abbey to certain tenements in Middlesbrough, even though they had been granted at the original foundation of Middlesbrough Priory.[19]

The Dissolution Accounts of Middlesbrough Priory make it clear that it was not particularly well endowed compared with some of the more famous monasteries of Yorkshire. Nevertheless, it had an important role to play in the history of Whitby Abbey. It was both a source of profit and a source of strife for the Abbots of Whitby, and although the tiny village of Middlesbrough must have been a rural backwater in the middle ages, the history of its priory could never be described as uneventful.

Notes and References

1. J C Atkinson, (ed) *Whitby Cartularly* Surtees Society (2 vols 1878-9) vol I p.95.
2. W Brown, (ed) *Guisborough Cartularly* (2 vols 1889-91) vol II, p.34.
3. *Whitby Cartularly* vol II, pp.95-116.
4. R L Kirby, *Ancient Middlesbrough* (1900) pp.62-69.
5. P Meadows 'In Great Ruyne & Deecaie': Middlesbrough Church in 1718' in *Bulletin of the Cleveland and Teesside Local History Society*, vol 60, (1991).
6. *Whitby Cartularly* vol II, p.370.
7. Cleveland and Teesside Local History Society, *The History of Middlesbrough in Maps* (1996 edition), Map I.
8. *Guisborough Cartularly* vol II, p.303.
9. *Guisborough Cartularly* vol II, p.34, and W Farrer (ed) Early Yorkshire Charters vol II (1916), No 703.
10. *Guisborough Cartularly* vol I, p.279.
11. *Guisborough Cartularly* vol II, p.416.
12. *Guisborough Cartularly* vol I, p.5.
13. *Whitby Cartularly* vol I, pp.214-216.
14. *Register of William Wickwane* Surtees Society vol 114 (1907), p.137, and *Victoria County History, Yorkshire* vol III, pp.102-3.
15. The following details of the story are taken from; WA Pantin *Documents Illustrating the Activities of the General and Provincial Chapters of the English Black Monks* Camden Third Series vol 45 (1937), pp.277-309.
16. *Calendar of Patent Rolls*, 1367-70, p.61.
17. *Calendar of Patent Rolls*, 1370-74, p.107.
18. *Calendar of Close Rolls*, 1392-96, p.92.
19. *Calendar of Close Rolls*, 1396-99, p.8.

10. STOCKTON CASTLE: GONE AND ALMOST FORGOTTEN

by Robert Woodhouse

REDEVELOPMENT SCHEMES HAVE TRANSFORMED MANY of our town centres and often the bulldozers have removed significant historical sites, but few locations have disappeared as completely as Stockton Castle. For centuries it was a favoured residence of the Bishops of Durham, where royal visitors were entertained in grand style amid orchards, parkland and ranges of buildings, but today there are few reminders of those glory days and the impressive stonework that covered a triangular shaped site between the modern Bridge Road and the river Tees.

It is unclear when land at Stockton was first acquired by the Bishops of Durham but during the late twelfth century, Bishop Hugh le Puiset became a major power in the land. Much of the church's wealth came from the sale of wool and a large proportion of this valuable product was produced in the Stockton area.

During the early thirteenth century, King John made several visits to Bishop Poicteu at Stockton and a charter granted by him to the burgesses of Newcastle-upon-Tyne is dated at Stockton on 5 February 1214. This riverside location by the Tees proved popular with successive bishops during the thirteenth century and on his retirement from office in 1249, Nicholas de Farnham retained use of the manor house at Stockton and spent much of the following eight years sampling the fresh air and fishing beside the Tees. Bishop Anthony Bek entertained King Edward I at Stockton on several occasions in the closing years of the thirteenth century. These occasions must have created quite a spectacle as the bishop's liveried retinue alone is said to have numbered some 140 officials and servants.

In the early fourteenth century several North East townships were damaged by Scottish raiders and it seems certain that Stockton suffered drastically when Robert Bruce and Sir James Douglas penetrated as far as the Tees in 1312, 1314 and again during 1316. Documentary references highlight rebuilding work carried out after this episode on the orders of Bishop Kellow and excavations on the site during 1969 verify the beautiful design work of masons at that time.

A survey of 1344, ordered by Bishop Thomas Hatfield, gives minute details of buildings and adjacent parkland and it seems likely that rebuilding work after the earlier Scottish raids led to the use of the term 'castle' rather than manor house. Correspondence from the period observes that the Bishop of Durham 'hath a fair house and his best provision at Stoketon-upon-Tese'.

Extensive and lengthy periods of rebuilding were carried out on the orders of Bishop Thomas Langley in the early 1400s. During his period of office between 1406 and 1437 he paid some eighty visits to his castle at Stockton and though there are no details for the remaining years of the fifteenth century, the buildings seem to have gone into a period of decline. Writing in the early 1530s, Leland places 'Stoketon-upon-Tese' amongst 'the market towns and castellies in Dirhamshire' but when an enquiry was made in 1574 into the condition of Stockton Castle it was described as being generally very 'decaied and ruynose'. The report included a detailed account of each building within the castle walls and indicated that a sum of around £1,600 was said to be needed for repair work. Further work was carried out on orders from Bishop Barnes but in 1597 part of the castle was destroyed by fire.

Stockton Castle's final demise began with the outbreak of hostilities during 1640. Royalist forces were defeated by Scottish troops at Newburn in August of that year and Bishop Morton fled to 'his castle at Stockton' before seeking a safer refuge in York and then London. A convention between English and Scottish forces in the form of the Treaty of Ripon, signed on 1 October 1640, stated that the river of Tees shall be the bounds of both armies, excepting always the town and estate of Stockton and the village of Egglescliffe; and that the counties of Durham and Northumberland be the limits within which the Scots army is to reside.

Although the Scots left the area in 1642, Royalist forces remained vigilant and the strategic position overlooking Yarm bridge was strengthened. The northern arch of the bridge was removed, to be replaced by a drawbridge, which was to be drawn up each night by the rector of Egglescliffe village, Dr Isaac Basire. On 1 February 1644, rival forces clashed on lowland to the west of the bridge and victims of this violent encounter were buried in local churchyards.

Stockton's support for the King's cause ended on 14 July 1644, when Scottish forces entered the town under the Earl of Callender. Charles the First's campaign in the North Country was halted at Marston Moor near York. Stockton Castle's fate was sealed by an Order of Parliament dated 14 October 1645. It stated that this and several other garrisons in the north 'Being placed there without the consent of both Houses of Parliament of England or their

Figure 1. The last surviving building from Stockton Castle. The barn stood on the corner of Bridge Road and Moat Street. *Author's collection*

Committees, may be speedily removed.' During 1646 Scottish forces still occupied Stockton Castle as well as other northern garrisons at Carlisle, Hartlepool and Tynemouth and it took considerable financial inducements before they withdrew.

A further Order of Parliament, made on 26 February 1647 states 'that Stockton Castle be made untenable and the garrison dismantled.' Five months later on 13 July, the House of Commons passed a resolution 'That the house doth concur with the Lords that the works about Stockton Castle made sithence these troubles be slighted and dismantled and the garrison dispersed.' Surveys made in 1647 testify to the ruinous state of the castle at this time:

> *That the Bishop's Castle situate at the south end of the town of Stockton by the rive Tease is ruinous and in great decay... thet the Castle hath a great moate about it, but the same is now, for want of cleansing, filled up in part and within that moate hath heretofore been orchards and gardens, but all destroyed. There hath likewise been a parke, but the same hath been disparked.*

After several years of occupancy by Scottish forces, the castle buildings and adjacent lands represented a sorry spectacle and on 24

March 1648, Stockton manor was sold to William Underwood and James Nelthorpe for £6,165 10s 2¹/₂d, but it was some years later before the stonework from the castle was totally removed.

One relic from the castle precincts survived until the mid 1860s. It was mentioned in one of the surveys of 1647 as 'The Barn' (Figure 1) 'which hath been lately built and is a very large one, built of stone and decays very little.' This 'embattled cowhouse' (as it was termed by the Durham historian Surtees) was sold on 29 June 1865 and pulled down soon afterwards.

Soon after the castle's demolition in the early 1650s, the township of Stockton was largely rebuilt. In 1661, Reverend Thomas Rudd recorded that of 120 dwelling houses in Stockton, none was built of brick or stone-clay walls and thatched roof only-and much of the castle's stonework seems to have been used in this late seventeenth century phase of redevelopment. Traces of 'dressed' stonework from the castle could be clearly seen in the lower levels of buildings along Castlegate, Finkle Street (Figure 2) and Tower Street before recent renewal schemes (since the 1970s).

One or two items from the castle have a fascinating history of their own. Two pillars of Frosterley marble were built into the walls of the

Figure 2. The buildings in Finkle Street were said to have been constructed with stone from the castle. *Author's collection*

Figure 3. The cottages on the corner of Castlegate and Bridge Road before demolition to make way for the Castle Theatre. This area was part of the castle site. *Author's collection*

barn after originating from the *Blue Posts Inn* built in 1485 on the west side of the High Street, following demolition of the barn, the pillars were bought by the Burdon family of Castle Eden and later they were transferred to Preston Hall Museum. Tucked away in a corner of Stockton's Green Dragon Heritage Centre is 'the Lion Stone' which is commonly known as the only identifiable remains of Stockton Castle and it has quite a chequered history of its own. After demolition of the castle in 1652, 'the Lion Stone' turned up in a farmyard at Hartburn belonging to a Mr G Sutton. From there it was removed to the grounds of Colonel Sleigh's residence at Elton where it was uncovered in the early 1920s, at a location in Crow Wood, marking the burial place of a famous racehorse, *Othello*. It was subsequently placed in the vestibule of the old Borough Hall (at the south end of the town's High Street) but when this building was demolished to make way for the Odeon Cinema (itself since demolished) and the General Post Office in the early 1930s, 'the Lion Stone' disappeared among the debris. In 1953 it was rediscovered in a heap of rubble at the north end of the lake in Ropner Park from where it was transferred first to Preston Hall Museum and then to the Green Dragon Heritage Centre.

The site of the castle precincts remained intact until well into the nineteenth century, with markings on the ground showing the line of the moat (which ran diagonally through the current Holy Trinity churchyard and roughly along the line of Castlegate opposite Yarm Lane). Subsequent redevelopment of this sector of land saw construction of two ivy clad cottages (close to the northern end of Bridge Road), (Figure 3) but they were, in turn, demolished to make way for the Castle Buildings. The foundation stone for the group of buildings was laid by Mrs Richard Murray of Elm Park, Harrogate, on 3 October 1907 and Mr William Kirk's company gave the first performance in the new theatre on Friday 31 July 1908. Press reports for the show *The Lady of Lyons* state that Mr Stork was 'supported by a talented company of lady and gentlemen amateurs.'

The new theatre was well supported in the late Edwardian period and a highlight was and appearance by local girl, Ivy Close, shortly after her success in a national beauty queen contest. She went on to star in Hollywood films but this trend towards moving pictures brought a decline in attendances. The theatre was subsequently reopened as the Empire and enjoyed great success under its licensee and manager Mr T H Burns. A contemporary report records that

> *the interior is most artistic and comfortable, and is one of the finest places of entertainment in the North of England.*

The advent of television brought a fall in cinema attendances and after a brief interlude as a bingo venture, the Empire finally closed its doors in the late 1960s. (The impressive block of buildings which fronted onto Castlegate and Bridge Road also included shops and a suite of billiard rooms). Again the site was cleared during the early months of 1970 in readiness for the construction of the Castle Centre (Figure 4).

Adjacent ground between Bridge Road and the riverside was covered by the Castle Brewery, which began operations under the Kirk brothers in the 1860s and was in the hands of J W Cameron Limited during its final phase in the early 1960s. Fragments of pottery, glass, roof tiles and clay pipes were uncovered along with ornate stonework and carved pillars while evidence of rebuilding schemes verified documentary reports of renewal after Scottish incursions. In spite of this work (and a recent excavation in John Walker Square prior to alterations to the Castle Centre) detailed evidence about the castle remains tantalizingly scarce.

Figure 4. Buildings in Castlegate on the route of the castle's northern perimeter. The properties were demolished in 1970. *Author's collection*

A fine lithograph of Stockton Castle in Brewster's history of the town, which shows a tall turreted frontage similar to the Bastille in Paris, was widely regarded as imaginative and inaccurate, but discovery of a front view sketch of the building in Oxford's Bodlian Library - produced as one of the surveys of 1647 – seems to give an amount of credence to Brewster's illustration. (The town's insignia showing a castle and anchor was certainly derived from this source (Figure 5).

Most old buildings attract a wealth of folklore and Stockton Castle is no exception. Perhaps the most persistent stories surround alleged tunnels from the castle precincts to various nearby locations, but in reality these tunnels either do not exist or were simply drains running in an easterly direction towards the Tees. In recent years there have been several incidents in the area of Yarm Lane and the High Street where the modern roadway has subsided to expose a large cavity. After careful investigation, these have turned out to be drains rather than tunnels. The most fanciful of these tales suggested a tunnel from the castle to Thornaby Green, but this would have involved a passage under the river and then running uphill to a considerable height above the Tees. Such a story may be totally dismissed; some castles did have a sally port – a short stretch of tunnel to allow defenders, in times of siege, to make their way from the castle precincts beyond the

Figure 5. The town's early insignia depicting a castle and anchor serves as a reminder of the Bishop of Durham's manor house or castle. *Author's collection*

THIS STONE COMMEMORATES
THE RE-OPENING OF THE OLDEST
SURVIVING GEORGIAN THEATRE.
ORIGINALLY OPENED IN 1766.
RE-OPENED BY COUNCILLOR
JIM COOKE MAYOR. 29 APRIL 1980.

Figure 6. Stonework from the Castle is said to have been included in the Georgian Theatre which was built on the site of the barn. *Author's collection*

besieging force. Local castles, such as Whorlton, Knaresborough and Mulgrave had such passages and a most striking example can be seen at St Andrews in Scotland.

Another tale that is linked to many local castles suggests that Cromwell's Parliamentary forces bombarded the buildings from a nearby vantage point. In the case of Stockton Castle, the artillery is said to have been sited on Thornaby Green. There was certainly plenty of activity in the Stockton and Yarm area during the English Civil War, but there is no foundation for such a story and although Scottish forces garrisoned the castle during hostilities, there is every likelihood that their takeover met with little resistance.

A more intriguing mystery surrounds the disappearance of stonework from the castle site. At its peak, this bishop's residence had several substantial ranges of buildings, and clearance of materials following demolition in the 1650s must have presented a major operation. An amount of stone was certainly reused in redevelopment of the town and as well as stonework in lower levels of properties in Finkle Street and Castlegate (before the 1970 programme of redevelopment) a series of dressed stones along the river banks were identified as having originated from the Castle site. Some buildings, such as the coffee shop in Finkle Street, the Georgian Theatre (Figure 6) in Theatre Yard and a wall of the old chapel in Bishop Street, are said to be constructed with stone from the castle, but it seems likely that large amounts of the stone were removed to outlying areas for re-use. No. 95 Hartburn Village is built of regular blocks of yellow Triassic sandstone, which probably originates from Stockton Castle, and experts have identified other amounts of decorated stone at properties on Hartburn Lane (opposite the western side of Ropner Park).

Few artifacts have been recovered from the site, but display cases at Cameron's Lion Brewery, Hartlepool, include a key cannonball and brick which is said to be from the castle.

My interest in Stockton Castle began in the early 1960s, when business premises in the High Street-Yarm Lane area included the Castle Hat Shop, the Castle Café and (former) Castle Theatre as well as the Castle Brewery on Bridge Road pointed to the existence of castle buildings in the locality. Since then, redevelopment of the site with the Castle Centre and the *Swallow Hotel* has ruled out further archaeological excavations for the time being, but who can say that a future round of redevelopment will not allow more attempts to unearth some of Stockton Castle's many secrets.

11. CLEVELAND CHEMICAL INDUSTRY

by David Tomlin

THE FIRST CHEMICAL INDUSTRY OF THE AREA was the Yorkshire Alum industry which operated from about 1600 to 1872. It worked the mineral in the hills and along the coast where the alum shales appeared in the geological strata. The shale was calcined in heaps with cheap fuel such as wood or poor quality coal. The material was then barrowed into stone walled tanks to be leached with water. The concentrated liquor was run from the tanks to the alum house for boiling (Figure 1). The alum crystallised out in the wooden barrels and was reprocessed away from the area in Newcastle or London. The by-product from this industry was Epsom salts (magnesium sulphate) which was a popular product from the chemist in the Victorian era. It is now to be found in bath salts, but everyone today uses skin soft detergents!

The modern chemical industry started in the lower Tees valley in 1833 at Urlay Nook near Egglescliffe and Yarm. This works was situated next to the recently arrived Stockton and Darlington Railway of 1825, and its influence continued over many decades and into the following centuries. They originally made fertilisers but in the twentieth century specialised in making chromium compounds. It is now an International Company named Elementis.

Middlesbrough, founded in 1830 by the extension of the railway down river from Stockton, developed a chemical industry in 1860

Figure 1. Sandsend Alum Quarries in 1814. *Prepared from a print by Walker*

with the foundation of a works by William Jones. This works was situated in Cargo Fleet Road. A newspaper report in the first year of operation said that 'the Guisborough Alum Company was setting up a works to make superphosphate of lime'. Other reports said they were making sulphuric acid from the iron pyrites found in another seam of strata with the Cleveland ironstone. At this period of time most sulphuric acid was made in Great Britain from pyrites, which was imported from other parts of the world. To make superphosphate, bones were reacted with sulphuric acid to make a synthetic fertiliser, the first one in common use in Europe.

Jones was soon controlled under the *Alkali Act*, which came into power in 1863 and was the first legislation which controlled environmental pollution. This works made alkali by the French La Blanc process and was the core of the chemical industry in that century. This was a two-step chemical process, the first where salt is reacted with sulphuric acid to make saltcake, the second is to mix coal and limestone with the saltcake to make black ash. This is dissolved in water and the soda goes into solution and can be crystallised out. The insoluble material, which could be a substantial amount of the mass, had to be thrown away as alkali waste had no use at that point in history. An early documentary source for the use of hydrochloric acid for the local textile industry can be found in Richmond in his book of 1868, the entry for May 1827 says:

> The Bleach works of T.A. Tennant at Stockton entered during the night and upwards of 1200 gallons of oxygenated muriatic acid destroyed, a reward of 20 guineas offered for the discovery of the offender or offenders.

Muriatic acid is the archaic name for hydrochloric acid.

The modern British chemical industry took off from about 1850, when there was a chemical understanding for those from university of some of the fundamental principles of modern chemistry. In 1856, Perkin first made a modern dye, but he did not know its chemical formulae. This started a revolution in both Germany and Great Britain to make new synthetic dyes from coal tar products. This term is still commonly used which confuses people who do not have a chemical degree. The raw material for these chemicals is now petroleum products. At the end of the 1860s, Mr Samuel Sadler arrived in the area and set up a chemical works in about 1875, next to Jones (Figure 2). The business grew from strength to strength for in 1882 he took over the Jones business and he continued to expand. The main raw materials were the coal tar from both the many gas works in the region and later the materials from the by-product coke ovens at

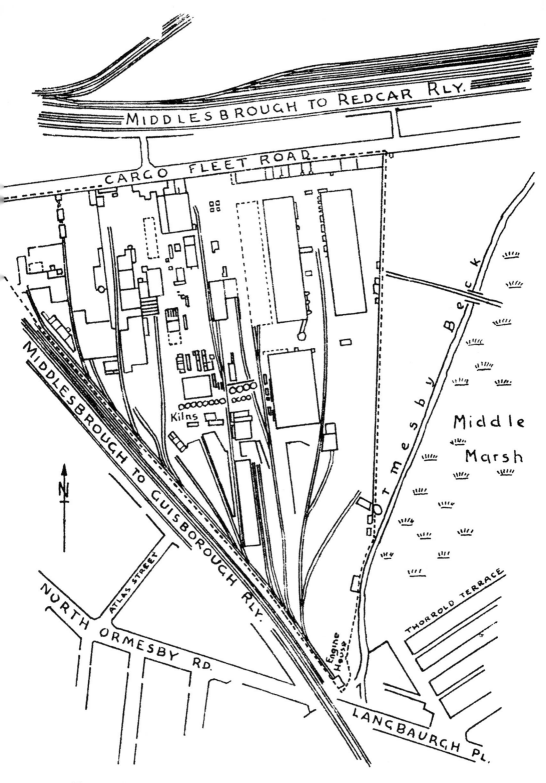

Figure 2. S A Saddler's Works at Cargo Fleet Road 1912. *Author's collection*

ironworks. Natural products such as bone and blood have been processed in the area and can be considered as a branch of the chemical industry. There was a bone mill next to the 1887 bridge at Stockton on the Thornaby side of the river. It must have presented an odiferous scent when travelling that way on the trams. Many letters appeared over the years in the local newspapers on this subject. Also coke ovens were built along the river to supply the improving technology of the local Blast Furnaces, such as at Port Clarence and Newport.

Salt Industry

The salt bed under the Tees estuary was discovered in 1862 at the Middlesbrough Iron works of Bolckow and Vaughan, near to where the Transporter bridge now stands. Bell Brothers at Port Clarence first exploited the salt bed in 1882 on the north side of the river. The peak of solid salt production was in 1894 when 314,000 tons were produced. Salt is still extracted by the brining method but today is used in its liquid form as a raw material by the chemical industry. The individual companies that operated in the area can be divided, for geographical simplicity, into south and north of the river. The Cleveland Salt Company and the Owners of the Middlesbrough Estate were on the south side of the river. North of the river around the Greatham we had what started as the Hartlepool Salt and Brine Company and finally was Cerebos which survived until 1971. Around the Port Clarence area was Bell Brothers, and in Haverton Hill there was C Tennant & Partners, C. Allhusen & Son, the Tees Salt Company, the South Durham Salt Company and the Eastfield Salt Company. The twentieth century began with the chemical industry in a thriving situation. Therefore in 1899 the local export of chemicals out of the river was:

Table 1

Salt	159,040 tons
Chemicals	27,954 tons
Basic Slag	53,584 tons

Source: Middlesbrough Chamber of Commerce (only copy, Middlesbrough Reference Library, Local Collection)

The basic slag was produced from the Basic Bessemer process for making steel. A company called H & E Alberts, ground the slag in the Ironmasters district of Middlesbrough, for local use and some went for export. The phosphate content of the Cleveland ironstone goes into the basic slag with this Bessemer process.

Figure 3. The Zinc Works at Seaton Carew 1950. *Author's collection*

The Twentieth Century

In the Cleveland area there was not much change for a few years in the new century. Industrial developments come in leaps and bounds but do not fit the historians time scale. The main impetus was the First World War when chemical weapons were first used, such as Mustard Gas. Luckily this area was not involved in either the invention or the production of these types of chemical materials. However, high explosive were produced in the area such as TNT and there were plans to make ammonium nitrate but they did not come to fruition until a few years after the First World War. Toluene, a distillate fraction from coal tar, was the raw material to make TNT. In this dangerous process the organic material was carefully reacted with a strong sulphuric/nitric acid mixture. As frequent accidents happened with this chemical reaction, the plant was built well away from habitation to avoid demolition of houses and killing people.

At the mouth of the river Tees at Seaton Carew, the Zinc Works appeared in the 1907-8 period (Figure 3). This works used mineral shipped from Australia. In its later years it was Leather Chemicals and they operated a lead chamber process for making sulphuric acid until 1972, the last such plant in the British Isles and this was filmed by the Open University.

Synthetic Ammonia and Nitrates 1920

The First World War caused a demand for ammonium nitrate explosive to put into armaments. At that point in history the source of the nitrate was the ' Chile nitrate' from that country in South America. The supply was being affected by the submarine war conducted by Germany. The Ministry of Munitions started a factory project at Billingham to make ammonium nitrate. The Germans had solved this problem just before the war by the invention of the Haber Bosch process in which synthetic ammonia could be made from air and coal. It was high-pressure technology leading the world, so that enabled the Germans to enter a war on a strong foundation.

The Brunner Mond staff from the north west of England came to Billingham but initially had great difficulty in obtaining information when they toured Germany. The Germans, who even stole notebooks from their baggage, sabotaged them. They first produced synthetic ammonia, at Christmas 1923 at Billingham plant. Initially ammonium sulphate was made as a general fertiliser for agricultural use. In the second half of the 1920s, anhydrite was produced from under the factory site at Billingham and this continued until the mine was closed in 1971. Anhydrite is a calcium sulphate with no water of crystallisation, which could be reacted with ammonia to make this fertiliser.

WORKSHOPS

PURGE GAS HOLDER

FIRE & AMBULANCE HUT

PROCESS OFFICE

NITROGEN GAS HOLDER

CO₂ GAS HOLDER

SULPHATE PLANT

WORKERS' CANTEEN

SULPHATE SILO

STAFF CANTEEN

DRAWING OFFICE

COMMERCIAL OFFICE

ACCOUNTS OFFICE

CHILTON'S LANE

STORES

BOILERS CEMENT STORE

CHALK DUMP

THE GRANGE

HAVERTON HILL ROAD

PORT CLARENCE BRANCH L.N.E.R.

ANHYDRITE DUMP

AMMONIA PLANT

SUB-STATION

GAS PLANT

FUEL DUMP

CATALYSED GAS HOLDER

WATER GAS HOLDER

1. Photograph of Site in 1926.

Figure 4. A view of the ICI site at Billingham in 1926. *Courtesy of ICI Archives, Synetix Chilton Site*

Imperial Chemical Industries 1926

In 1926 a number of British companies jointed together to supply the British Empire with chemical products (Figure 4). This was the combination of Brunner Mond, United Alkali, British Dyestuffs Corporation and Nobel Industries. Sir Harry McGowan signed the final agreement on a transatlantic liner.

If it was not for the financial strength of ICI the Billingham plants could easily have closed in the general industrial gloom and doom of the 1930s after the Wall Street crash of 1929. In the early 1930s all the shipyards in the Stockton area closed for good and caused problems in the associated engineering industries.

In 1935 ICI started to make synthetic petrol from creosote and coal dust and this operated into the war years and provided high-octane fuel for the RAF. This plant was modified after the war and made plasticiser alcohols which went in PVC etc and continued in operation until 1994.

Tioxide

Another company to appear between the wars was British Titan Products, which was later known as Tioxide International Ltd. This factory started in 1934 to produce titanium dioxide, which was then a new substitute for white lead in paint, a much safer chemical non-toxic substance. In 1963 they opened new laboratories in Portrack Lane in Stockton. A new plant at Greatham was opened in 1971 to make the titanium dioxide via the chloride route, a new chemical process for this area. A further development of the chloride process occurred in 1977 when £2 M grant from the Government was paid to this company. The newspaper report of 21 January said that the accelerated project grants were devised to encourage companies to bring forward major projects at a time of severe economic depression. So there were economic problems in this sector of the chemical industry from this statement.

In 1990, ICI, already owning half of Tioxide, bought the other half share from the Cookson Group. In 1993 it was reported that the company had ten factories worldwide and that nearly 500 were employed at Greatham and 350 at the Haverton Hill Road site, which is in Billingham. (Subsequently this is now Huntsman Tioxide)

The Second World War

Many of the local industries went over to the war effort during the 1939 to 1945 period. This especially applied to ICI at Billingham, which operated its own secret naming of projects such as PIAT and TUBE ALLOYS.

The PIAT was an anti-tank weapon, which was successfully designed at Billingham. Then even more interesting was TUBE ALLOYS which was the secret name for the preliminary studies to produce minerals for nuclear weapons, but this was developed in other areas, such as the USA. The plant that was finally built after that war was Sellafield, on the west coast of England. The Government in its early decades managed that by the Ministry of Supply. Only in recent years has it become a private commercial company at arms length from the Government, namely BNFL (British Nuclear Fuels Ltd).

Petrochemical Age

The main company to develop this technology in this area was ICI The Petrochemical industry had developed in the U.S.A., between the wars, but had little influence in the U.K., with its plentiful supply of cheap coal tar from gas works and coke ovens. After the war, the Petrochemical industry slowly came into various regions of the British Isles, especially near deepwater ports where the oil raw materials, could be brought in at a low price from any part of the world. At this time British Petroleum had a major refinery in the Persian Gulf and could supply the UK market. This all changed with political changes in that region.

The petrochemical age took off in the USA, presumably because of the great popularity of the mass-produced motorcar, led by Henry Ford. The spin off was the by-products from the distillation in the oil refineries. They started making synthetic alcohol and glycols, which the UK continued to make from natural products (vegetable materials) right into the 1950s when the economics of that process killed that method off.

Today, distillate fractions and synthetic chemicals, from the petroleum industry now replace many materials that are labelled 'coal tar products'.

ICI Wilton

In the second half of the 1940s, ICI worked with Eston Urban District Council to establish a very large manufacturing site on the south side of the river. The company bought the Wilton country estate from the Lowther family in 1946. They only needed the flat land near the river, south of the Redcar trunk road but had to buy the whole of the estate, which included the hillside, the castle

Figure 5. Wilton Castle, bought by ICI as part of the Lowther estate. *Courtesy of ICI Archives, Synetix Chilton Site*

(Figure 5) and the farms. The first plants built in 1949 were the phenol/ formaldehyde and the perspex plants, both plastic materials. The plastic age had begun for this area a few years before with a perspex plant at Billingham in the war (Figure 6).

The first olefines plant, a craker, started in 1951, producing 35,000 tons of ethylene a year. This is really small by today's standards, and this type of plant remains at the core of chemical production (Figure 7).

In the early 1970s the site contained Dyestuffs Division with the Nylon 66 polymer plant with a capacity of 110,000 tons per year. Nylon was obviously used in textiles and carpets. Another divisional product was Lissapol N, a liquid detergent made from ethylene oxide. Also the alkylphenol plant was built around this decade. Polyether made from propylene oxide for polyurethane foams. The aniline plants were also constructed and operated successfully. Heavy Organic Chemicals Division, had olefines, butadiene, propylene oxide and ethylene glycol. Also plants to make ethylene, ethylene oxide, ethylene glycol, para-xylene and phthalic anhydride. Mond Division made chlorine from common salt and titanium metal via the chloride route. Plastics Division made alkathene, propathene and Transpex. There was also a Fibres Division that made terylene, a revolutionary new textile component.

In the 1980s the company was active in the International market wheeling and dealing. In February 1986, it was announced in the company newspaper that they had reached agreement with EniChem of Italy for a joint venture. This scheme involved the vinyl chloride monomer (VCM) and polyvinyl chloride (PVC) business. The agreement included the planned removal, over a period of some two years of around 300,000 tonnes of both VCM and PVC capacity, equivalent to up to half of the then current excess of West European capacity. The joint venture would then have VCM capacity of 1.2 million tons and PVC of one million tons and should be able to operate at very high plant loading. The main use of PVC was the insulating plastic on electrical cables.

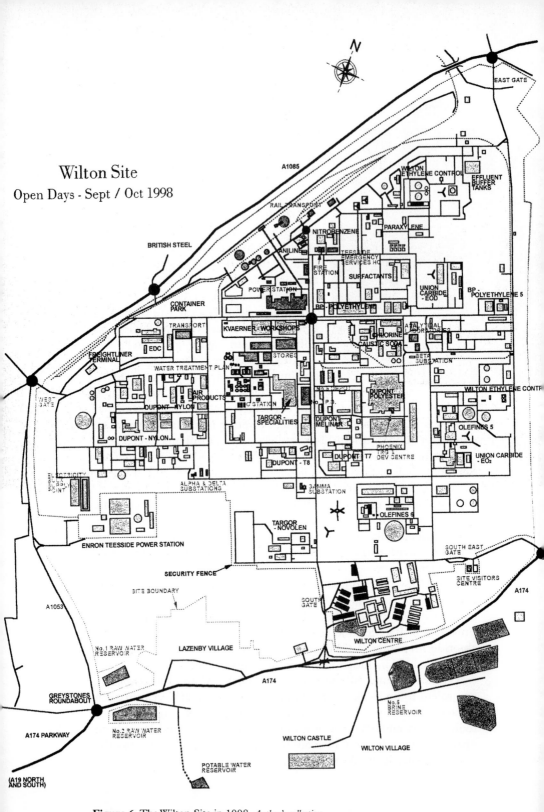

Figure 6. The Wilton Site in 1998. *Author's collection*

Figure 7. ICI's Olefines Plant at Wilton. *Courtesy of ICI Archives, Synetix Chilton Site*

Oil Refineries

Surprisingly no oil refineries were built on the Tees estuary just after the Second World War. There was British owned oil capacity in many parts of the world. Political changes in the 1950s also caused changes in the world production of chemicals.

In the 1960s two oil refineries were built on opposite sides of the river. Phillips Imperial Petroleum refinery primary function was to provide naptha for the ICI crackers at Wilton and as a spin off local people could buy cheap Imperial petrol for their cars.

Phillips Petroleum whose home base is Bartleville, Oklahoma had expanded their oil refinery capacity over the years. In the mid 1970s there was a big expansion at Seal Sands where primary distillation units were built to process the crude oil which came from the Ekcofisk sector of the North Sea in Norwegian waters.

The *Evening Gazette* reported in 1992 that:

Teesside's only oil refinery is busy with good demand and managers are cautiously optimistic about the future. The firm, which employs 220 people, processes about 4.5 million tonnes of oil at its North Tees refinery, Billingham.

In 1967 Shell built a refinery near to the newly developing Tees Dock, a deep-water facility of the Tees and Hartlepool Port Authority. This closed in 1984, and the plant and equipment was dismantled and sold on the world market. A truly unusual industrial event in that this refinery lasted only seventeen years. The refinery's demise was partly due to its small size compared with other similar UK installations.

A spin off from refineries is the handling of many gases and a company to come to the area was Air Products. They have subsequently bought into the chemical production side of the industry in the last decades of the twentieth century.

Seal Sands Chemical Park
The Tees and Hartlepool Port Authority had reclaimed major parts of the Tees estuary over many decades. In the late 1960s an expansion occurred with the arrival of Rohm and Haas making acrylics. The English common name is perspex but in the States it is called plexiglass. Also Monsanto built a plant to make acrylonitrile and that raw material could be shipped to other parts of Europe for further processing to make acrylan for synthetic fibres. This was used in clothes and carpets. It was reported that Monsanto employed 230 people in 1976 at its Seal Sands complex. At that time they showed a 61 per cent increase in net income for the first quarter of the year compared with the same period of 1975. This plant was sold to BASF in the 1980s and they continue to operate an acrylonitrile plant and other chemical plants which have been built on that site.

The Rohm and Haas site has been demolished and the site is occupied by Fine Organics which was owned by Laporte.

Hampshire Chemicals, an American owned company, has occupied a site next to BASF. This plant used hydrocyanic acid via a pipe through the boundary fence between the two company's works. They make complex organic compounds which are used in many industries.

Lundbeck, a Danish pharmaceutical company, bought the Prom plant at Seal Sands and has quietly expanded its production of very specialist chemicals.

The landing of natural gas by the Central Area Transmission

System (CATS) has encouraged a spin off, in the form of electrical power stations. The Enron Corporation of Texas built a combined electrical power and steam station at Wilton. This base load for the gas supply has ensured gas for many industries in the Tees valley.

The Last Decade of the Twentieth Century

Mr Hanson must have had some influence on the dramatic events with the rationalisation that occurred in the 1990s. Hanson Trust bought a quantity of shares in ICI in the early years of the decade. His plan was to take over the company, rationalise it and sell on parts of the business at a profit, but he failed. Then ICI started to rationalise its business in certain chemical areas and this has continued over many years.

The result of this is that, DuPont, an American company, took over the Nylon works at Wilton on 1 July 1993. The raw materials to make nylon are cyclohexane, air and ammonia. After a number of processes nylon 66 salt is produced which is then polymerised and made into chips which can be transported to anywhere in the world.

The BASF flag was officially raised outside the Wilton Propathene 5 plant on the 1 March 1994. This is a company of German foundation and makes many chemicals for the world market. Propathene is a plastic material with many modern uses.

Union Carbide announced in December 1994 that it would take over ICI European ethylene glycol, ethanolamines, glycol ethers and brake fluids businesses. This has now changed its name in 2001 to Dow Chemicals in a partnership with the other company.

British Petroleum was involved with ICI in a polyethylene plant since 1982 and took complete control in November 1996. It has owned a twenty per cent share in the Wilton 'craker' for many years. In 1997 BASF announced they were in partnership with Hoesch to form, TARGOR which would operate the Novolene plant at Wilton, the former ICI owned plant.

The Last Years of the Century

The Albermarle Corporation on 2 November 1998 acquired the Teesport works of the Hodgson Speciality Chemicals division of BTP plc. The chemical industry was a world wide manufacturing complex and companies change ownership every year or so. Albermarle headquarters is in Richmond, Virginia, USA.

Avecia was the name change in September 1999 for what was Astra Zeneca a spin off from the 1990s ICI. Locally this involved the DTBA plant at Seal Sands.

In the 1990s the ICI Company split into two and issued two packages of shares to their shareholders. The second part was named Zenica which specialised in the pharmaceutical side of the world wide chemical industry.

Since its formation in 1998, INEOS has acquired a number of worldwide businesses.

The Twenty First Century

On 28 February 2001, INEOS announced that it was to axe two plants at Wilton which employed 105 people. In recent years the company had bought ICI Acrylics at Billingham and Bonar Polymers at Newton Aycliffe. Other changes were occurring with many companies. For example Hampshire was taken over by Dow Chemicals. Months later this company took over Chemoxy at the geographical core, Middlesbrough, of our area.

'A new name is making its presence felt on Teesside' announced the Evening Gazette on 19 June 2001, and that was PETROPLUS. Six months previously, this Dutch oil and gas storage company acquired the North Tees refinery of Philips Imperial. Surprisingly the name 'Imperial' is still used on some petrol retail garages certainly in the Teesside area.

This year (2001) Methanex, a Canadian based company took over complete control of the former ICI methanol plant at Billingham.

The Past-Some Conclusions

The chemical industry has always been in a dynamic situation but the rate of change is increasing with time. The change of ownership of many businesses is occurring even faster in the twenty-first century. The industry has always changed the materials that it manufactured; the nineteenth century was based on soda and sulphuric acid. Most of the twentieth century has been involved with plastics and synthetic fibres, so replacing many of the traditional materials like cotton and wool, used in garments manufacture. The chemical industry has its influence in many parts of the market place and has always been very active and aggressive.

This is only a brief description of the Cleveland chemical industry, but it has been around for a long time, namely 400 years. The alum industry, a craft trade, lasted the longest, 270 years from approximately 1600 to 1872. The Alkali Trade was the very core, the mainstay of the nineteenth century British chemical industry, but the only local company that operated this process was William Jones at Middlesbrough. As a result the Cleveland Chemical Industry is hardly mentioned in standard textbooks on the nineteenth century chemical industry. It has sadly been overlooked by the academics working in their ivory towers some miles away in the next County.

Author's Note

There are a number of pitfalls for similar named companies:

BITMAC and BRITMAG

The *Evening Gazette* said on 16 June 2000 that the Pittsburgh had acquired BITMAC, which employed eighty, at its Port Clarence works based coal tar chemicals company, Koppers Industries.

BRITMAG is a British company operating the magnesium from seawater plant at Hartlepool. More information can be found on the web page www.britmag.co.uk.

BTP and BTP

BTP was the short name of British Titan Products in the 1930s.
In the 1990s BTP stands for British Tar Products.
Now that is a real confusion!

Sources

1. *The Alum Industry*, Cleveland Industrial Archaeologist No 2 1975.
2. *The Early Chemical Works of Teesside*, D M Tomlin, Cleveland Industrial Archaeologist CIA No 4 1975.
3. *The Bore Holes and Salt Works of the Tees Estuary*, D M Tomlin CIA No 7 1977.
4. *The Cleveland Salt Company*, D M Tomlin CIA No 9 1978.

12. VIKING DESCENT: THE BULMERS OF WILTON-IN-CLEVELAND CASTLE

by Peter Davison

THE FIRST RECORDED BULMER was the Anglo-Scandinavian Anskitel, Sheriff of Yorkshire and survivor of the depredations of the Conqueror and his sons. Four hundred years later his descendant, Sir John Bulmer, (Figure 1) faced an equally ruthless foe, Henry VIII, who also descended from Anskitel.

Sir John succeeded to the estates in 1532, having had previous useful experience, including being a commissioner of the peace and, from 1529-32, Sheriff of Durham. However, whilst the Bulmer role on the Scottish borders had led to his father, Sir William's, almost hero status, for Sir John it led to a very dangerous enmity. There, the Duke of Norfolk (Figure 2) 'under a mere pretence of military offence – took away Sir

Figure 1. (right) The Bulmer Coat of Arms and Crest. The two main colours are red and gold. *Author's collection*

Figure 2. (below) The Duke of Norfolk Henry VIII's right hand man in suppressing the Pilgrimage of Grace. *By permission of the Lord Chamberlain, St James's Palace*

John's command,' thereby causing him considerable humiliation. As a result 'Sir John became, henceforth, the Duke's active enemy.'[1] Nevertheless, on 16 March 1535, at the time of the siege of Maynothe in Ireland, Thomas Fitzsyman wrote to Thomas Cromwell, the Chancellor, and 'Advises the King to send 100 or a half of Northern spears with Mr Bowmer, who was here before.'[2]

Another paper of the period fully names Sir John, In Monastic chan. Proceedings, 1533-39, he

> *had a house at Lastingham in 1528 when he was forbidden to kill deer in the Ward of Pickering forest and he also held Riseborough in the Vale of Pickering.*
>
> *One Sir John Bulmer of Wylton in Yorks. Kt, has entered into a parcel of the manor and there hath cut down divers great trees and woods, within the manor, has broken certain parcels of ground to take out STONES for his building and daily cauthes divers tenants of your orator, to deny their rents – and customs etc.*

Local historian, R H Hayes, my informant, adds, 'This must refer to Sir J B building his house with Towers?'[3]

Judging by the amount of time Sir John was in his Lastingham home in 1536-37, it must have been his favourite residence! The building of the house was, anyway, a cause of controversy to which Sir John was no stranger. Allegedly, on 8 October 1515, near Guisborough, Sir John Bulmer, with others, had assaulted and put in fear for his life, Christopher Conyers, supposedly at the instigation of the Prior of Guisborough, who was 'gretly ayded by many gret gentylmen of the same countre in his wronnges.'

Sir John, it seems, was hawking at North Cote that evening when Conyers appeared. An argument arose, with Conyers saying, 'Ye have bene ever agayn me, and all is for yone prior sake.' He drew his sword and Sir John struck him on the neck with the flat of his blade. The two were separated and Sir John said, 'Cosyn go your way.' Conyers retorted, 'Fye on your cosynage.' And Sir John continued, 'I will do you no wrong.' The truth is difficult to untangle, as there are contradictions. Prior Spyres meanwhile denied involvement, adding, 'Sir John never had any fee of him for berying or mayntenance in this matter, or any other his unlawfull causez.'[4]

Whilst Sir John had experience to prepare him for office, his temperament was questionable. Sister-in-law, Anne Bulmer, described him and her husband, Ralph, as 'something hasty'[5] and a modern historian sees him as 'of a generally nervous disposition.'[6]

His relationships also invited controversy. His presumably

arranged child-marriage to Anne Bigod was usual, with all but one of their offspring 'married before 1530, when he was not much over forty.'[7] The children were Ralph, William, Anne (Boynton), Elizabeth (Newton), Agnes (Layton) and Mary. However, by 1536 he had apparently 'bought'[8] and married Margaret, his mistress and former 'wife of William Cheyne late of London esq,'[9] though the authorities did not recognise the marriage. Whatever, they were a devoted couple and Sir John was adamant she was his wife, and their son, John, born in 1537, stated in 1584 that he was born in wedlock. Their daughters Anne, Maria and Francisca were, though, born before the marriage.

Margaret has been described as the 'illegitimate daughter of Edw(ard) Stafford, du(ke) of Buckingham'[10] (executed in 1521), but son John told the 1584 visitation that she was 'the illegitimate daughter of 'Henry' Stafford.'[11] Margaret was a colourful character with whom things did not come in half measure. Stunningly attractive but with a violent temper, she too had no love for the Duke of Norfolk, who was married to her half sister and who, she felt, had not tried sufficiently to try to save the Duke of Buckingham. Norfolk, in turn, felt 'her loud and virulent denunciations to be obnoxious.'[12]

Now Margaret and Sir John were to be thrust into a turbulence requiring cool heads. And the Duke would be watching closely.

Henry VIII broke with Catholicism and became head of the English Church in order to divorce Catherine of Aragon and marry Ann Boleyn. Meanwhile, Henry and England being in financial straits, commissioners conveniently found that monasteries were not functioning properly and a lucrative closure programme began. A mixture of fury and distress resulted, especially in the conservative and independent north. And whatever stirrings erupted the Bulmer brothers were bound to be involved, with Sir William the Constable of Wilton Castle, Sir John Steward of Guisborough Priory and Sir Ralph influential in Swaledale, as well as Bulmer office in Norham castle on the Tweed.

A letter from Christopher Lord Conyers and Sir John Bulmer reveals rumblings in Guisborough (Figure 3):

> *On Sunday, 11 July, at Gysburn in Yorkshire, when the parish priest was declaring the articles directed by the King to the Archbishop of York, one John Atkynson alias Brotton 'came violently and took book furth of the' priest's hands, and pulled it in pieces.*[13]

Prior Cocherell's resignation and replacement by Robert Silvester (alias Pursglove) can hardly have helped.

Rebellion began in Louth, Lincolnshire, with demands for re-

Figure 3. The ruins of Guisborough Priory showing how impressive this building once was. *Author's collection*

opening of monasteries, an end to peacetime tax and the exclusion of the king's unpopular advisers. The gentry seem to have been forced into involvement; their support did not last long and the rising ceased on 18 October 1536. Despite the limited threat, the King demanded 'terrible example'[14] should there be recurrence.

Meanwhile, stirrings erupted in Yorkshire with meetings at Beverley and Richmond on 7 and 11 October, and at Market Weighton on 13 October; that day Henry wrote to Sir Ralph Ellerker about the arrest of traitors and including Sir John Bulmer amongst those officials to be contacted. And by 16 October objectors from all over the North reached York, including Lords Neville, Lumley and Latimer. Government representatives seemed to have dithered and perhaps sympathised.

Protesters were required to swear the 'Oath of the Honourable Men,'[15] emphasising the religious cause, calling for the restoration of catholicism, the suppression of 'Heretics,' expressing loyalty to the King and calling for the expulsion of 'all villein blood and evil councillors from his Grace and Privy Council.' This was composed at York on 17 October by the emerging leader, Robert Aske, lawyer and, perhaps, in-law relation of Sir Ralph Bulmer.

Around 30,000 Pilgrims, now including more northern gentry such as Sir John and, as a Durham leader, Sir William Bulmer, plus abbots, next reached Pontefract. By 21 October Lord Darcy had surrendered the castle and became a Pilgrim leader, though he dreaded it he thought 'Old Tom had one traitor's tooth in his head.'[16] The authorities were not to be so persuaded. Seeing that the Durham leaders wore the Badge of the Five Wounds of Christ, Darcy distributed a collection of these he had from his Moorish campaign in Spain. The Durham group also carried St Cuthbert's banner. Six days later about thirty of the rebels, including Sir John Bulmer, Sir Robert Constable and Lords Darcy, Latimer and Lumley, met a similar number of royal representatives on a bridge over the Don to air the Pilgrim grievances. The meeting dragged and the impatient commons suspected their leaders of treachery. Sir Ralph Bulmer joined the Pilgrims later, having been with a company of men at an eight to ten thousand strong gathering with Lord Latimer at Bishop Auckland and also part of a force trying to seize royalist Skipton Castle. Meanwhile, former Prior Cockerill claimed that on about 11 November Sir Francis Bigod 'rose the country to bring him back to Guisborough,' complaint being that Prior Pursglove 'was not chosed formally, according to the laws of God and the old customs.'[17] And on 22 November the Council at York told Sir John Bulmer to ensure that Pursglove could be effective. Next, on 13 December, Pursglove asked for Sir John to come and advise, or, failing him, Sir William to visit, 'as several of the brethren' – were – 'using themselves very unreligiously.'[18]

Sir William Bulmer and Sir John's son, Ralph, were at a Pilgrim Council at Pontrefract, apparently from Saturday 2-4 December, when Sir Ralph and others took a list of grievances to Norfolk at Doncaster. Nevertheless, a pardon of about 8 December was distrusted, as were the gentry. And Sir Ralph Bulmer (Swaledale) and Sir John (Cleveland) and others, were to cool their districts. That unrest continued is indicated in a letter from Sir Marmaduke Constable to Cromwell of 11 January 1537, which described

Beverley and the East Riding as calm but the North Riding as 'still dangerous,'[19] also, the following day, Aske sent the King a letter warning of stirrings. The greatest threat was Bigod, who doubted the pardon and warned of betrayal by the gentry and of Norfolk's bringing a large force north. And, it seems, Bigod's wife tried to enlist the support of her uncle, Sir John Bulmer. No Bulmers were apparently involved, however, in the popular but unsuccessful attempt to take Scarborough, Beverley, where Bigod made his escape, and Hull, where John Hallam gallantly sacrificed himself, though Lord Lumley's son, George, was implicated. The King now withdrew the pardon and about two hundred were executed, including Robert Aske. At this stage, though, Sir John Bulmer seems to have been relatively secure. In a letter of 11 January, Sir Ralph Evers told him that the King's pardon was genuine and that Sir John's 'diligent service' had been reported. Pressure of work prevented his delivering 'a letter' – 'the King determined him.' Also, Sir John or Sir William were to go to Doncaster, where Norfolk would be at the end of January. He concluded, 'I pray you have me recommended to my lady your wife.'[20] Sir William Bulmer carried out the mission.

Shortly afterwards, Matthew Boynton informed Sir John that the authorities wished him to go to Cleveland to calm the district in anticipation of a move there by Bigod, whose capture would impress the King. He ended, 'From Barriston by your loving son-in-law' – signature – 'Sor, I besech you cyp the latter clos.'[21] Sir John wrote from Lastingham that the letter had arrived too late for him to act on and queried, anxiously, why he had not heard from the Duke of Norfolk and asked where people stood with the authorities. Later, when in prison, Sir John stated, 'I laid in waite for him' – Bigod – 'in Blacamayre and Cleveland but could not meet him.'[22] Meanwhile, Sir John had been awaiting word about the King's plans from his son, Ralph, in London. Volatility was indicated by the arrest of two of Bigod messengers on 17 January in Swaledale and Sir William Bulmer wrote to Sir John on 25 January, first congratulating Sir John and his wife on the birth of a son, then speaking of trouble originating with a Stokesley bill, which proposed the commons meet at the 'Hamellton Hills'. The gentry had no choice but to join, insisting, however, on peaceful, Pilgrimage 'order' behaviour. Also, he wrote, Prior Pursglove had said that the Duke of Norfolk would be in York on the following Monday.[23] Sir Robert Bowes suppressed the Cleveland unrest, causing Cromwell's agent, Sir Ralph Sadler, to comment therefore that the gentry could have suppressed the previous disorder. Sadler was at Wilton Castle from 23 to 28 January and not long afterwards Sir John wrote to his brother, Sir William, of alarming news:

> *Thomas Fulthorpe, Ralph's servant, came to me this afternoon and showed me Ralph sent word that the King has rigged thirty ships to come upon us, that my Lord Norfolk is coming down, that Aske has accused divers persons, and that Sir George Darcy has accused his father and Sir Robert Constable. His counsel is that neither you nor I stir out of the country 'for no fair letters nor words' see that watch be laid along the coast and that the beacons be ready, for I fear it is high time.*[24]

On 28 January, however, Gregory Conyers had written, reassuring Sir John of the continuance of the pardon and that the King would learn who calmed unrest. Sir John seems to have tried to keep his options open in this confusing climate; whilst trying to steady the commons he would gather 'treasonable bills' and his servants would observe. And some revealing bills were circulating. A paper from Kendal stated that the motives of the upper classes were religious, whilst the commons would assist them if there were concessions over rent, etc. Sir John was 'asked how he liked it' and he replied,

> *Marry, very well, for when two dogs fight for a bone the third will take it up; for this will make the gentlemen and commons fall forth, and the King shall take up the matter.*

And a southern 'bill' warned, 'Good Northern men, stick to your matter, for the Lord Norfolk comes to beguile you.'[25] Meanwhile, Bigod tantalisingly schemed that the commons abduct their local gentry, with Sir William Bulmer taken by Clevelanders and Sir John by Pickering and Blackmoor commons. A staged rising in Richmondshire would coincide with Norfolk's arrival in Doncaster and lure him north without his main force. Clevelanders would then seize him 'about Byland.'[26]

Another version proposed Sir John go to Wilton and be taken by Guisborough commons, prior to his and their capturing Norfolk. The upper classes would co-operate with this on pain of death. His wife, Margaret, was aware of the scheme: 'She said divers times that if the Duke's head were off, Sir Ralph Evers' and Sir Ralph Ellerkers' men might go where they would.'[27]

En route to meeting Norfolk, Sir William called in at Lastingham, advised Sir John to lie low and received the bills he had gathered, to show the Duke. Sir John now began to quash the unrest. Sir Francis

Bigod had been captured in the Lake District on 4 February but this did not lead to the end of unrest. Norfolk and Suffolk were exacting revenge in Lincolnshire and there were serious doubts about the amnesty. Perhaps implicated by Gregory Conyers, Sir John and Margaret in mid-March received the dread summons to London. Any relief at Norfolk's allowing a postponement to Easter must have been dashed when, about 25 March (Palm Sunday), word came from Ralph that Sir John 'should look well to himself, for as far as he could perceive all was falsehood that they were dealt withall.'[28] Sir John Watts, Priest of Easington, captured the torment of the couple, with their new baby:

> *She is feared that she will be departed from him for ever... she peradventure will say, 'Mr Bulmer for my sake break a spear', and then he like a dow will* (say), *'Pretty Peg, I will never forsake thee.'*

His servants heard him say that 'he had liever be racked than part from his wife,' and she – 'declared that she would liever be torn in pieces than go to London.'[29] The Dodds feel, in reality Margaret encouraged Sir John to flee, while he declared, 'As good be slain and die in the field as be martyred as many other were above.'[30] And now, despite being a 'particularly unsuitable conspirator,'[31] Sir John embarked on his plot, thereby sealing both their fates. Local priests would be sounded out whether 'men's confessions'[32] suggested they might rebel and join in the seizure of Scarborough Castle 'on Easter Day,'[33] which was imminent. Accordingly, on the day before Good Friday, William Staynhus, the Bulmer's chaplain, left Lastingham, Margaret having proposed he see a former Pilgrim captain, Parson Franke, at Loftus, as well as Bartholomew Cottam. Parson Watts of Easington, Hinderwell's incumbent and possibly Gregory Conyers were to be seen, too. Having failed with Cottam and Watts, Staynhus continued to Loftus but Watts reached the 'marvellous witted' Franke first and informed him. Despite Franke's urgings, Staynhus discovered the two together. And Franke would only hear the message with the constable and bailiff present and said that Sir John had visited Lord Lumley, 'saying he had both brewed and baked and slain his beefs, and suddenly my Lord Lumley is gone.' Staynhus now withheld the original message and simply asked if Sir John and Margaret might avoid the summons to London. Franke retorted impatiently that Sir John should 'go as he is commanded.'[34] Destroying the letter, Staynhus departed with Watts, asking of the likely fate of those called to London. Watts' replied, 'All false harlots should be hanged by the neck.' Further help from Lumley was unlikely and Staynhus should 'beware fall not in love with her, for if ye do ye will be made as wise as your master and both will be hanged then.' Staynhus responded, 'I never wist she loved me but of late,' ie I was never on friendly terms with her until lately. Watts continued that he should persuade Sir John to take care and take care himself or face execution, as Sir John would have no support. Staynhus, though, felt that, failing an immediate commons rising, Sir John would 'flee to Ireland' in the hope of soon recovering his territories.[35] Finally, Watts told Staynhus he would be executed; and he was left in turmoil over 'this hideous and parlous case which passeth my rude understanding.'[36]

Meanwhile, Kirby-in-Cleveland's parson had been sounded out by Robert Hugill, and, just before Good Friday, Sir John had indeed visited Lord Lumley who, to 'great murmur,'[37] had vanished. Despite feeling any force of theirs could not resist Henry, Sir John wanted them to work together. With his son under arrest Lumley had worries of his own, however, and he apparently said that if he was ordered to the capital 'he would bring 10,000 at his tail'[38] and also commented that 'Sir John Bulmer was one of the chief causers of the last commotion in Cleveland.'[39]

Strangeways, Latimer, Darcy and, perhaps, Constable were also unresponsive, though it is likely they were en route to the capital. So, with Staynhus in Loftus, a probably frantic Sir John visited his holding of Rosedale Abbey, where the parson, Sir James Otterburn, spoke of Norfolk's severity and hinted that rebellion was in the air. Consolation also came with a letter from the royalist Sir Ralph Evers, strongly criticising Cromwell, though Evers, disbelieved by Norfolk, claimed this to be forged. Nevertheless, Sir John was arrested, apparently in Lastingham. Margaret left for London on 8 April; the dreaded separation had occurred. And on the same date 'Norfolk and others' sent word: 'Sends the confessions' concerning Sir John Bulmer, his pretended wife (Figure 4).

On the Duke's return to Sheriff Hutton he will send such other persons as he is instructed and with Sir John Bulmer shall come Sir Ralph Evers. Newcastle upon Tyne, 8 April.[40]

Sir John Bulmer rejoined his wife on about 21 April and the couple appear in Tower Records: 'Sir John Bulmer and his wife for 6 weeks at 20s.'[41] Also a letter of 25 April from John Husee in London states: 'The Tower is replenished with the Northern people, among which is the lady Bulmer with diverse abbots, priests, and priors.'[42]

Sir William Bulmer now visited Norfolk at Newcastle for reassurance. Norfolk wrote to Cromwell on 11 April; he felt that Sir

Figure 4. An engraving showing the arrest of the Bulmers by GE Pallant Sidaway. *Author's collection*

William was innocent:

> *we have heard that at the stirring in Cleveland he tried to stay the people. At the first commotion he said openly that if the King came or sent against them he would join his Highness. So we cannot find but that he is a true man. He repairs to London to the term and he desires me to write to you to be his good Lord, which I desire you to be if you cannot determine ill matter against him.*[43]

Sir William also appears in Tower Records as 'Pardoned and released'[44] but Sir John, Margaret and Ralph Bulmer were charged with 'treason and conspiracy against the King.'[45] The charges had to be validated by a local jury and Norfolk refers to these in a revealing letter of 10 May to the King:

> *Yesterday, at my being at York, was the greatest assembly of the gentlemen of this shire there had been seen these 40 years, – and – 'with very few exceptions they are very near of kin to those indicted. Sir James Strangewaies – 'near of kin to Bygod and Bulmer: Sir Henry Savell, Sir George Conyers -near of kin to Bulmer – Matthew Boynton – married to Sir John Bulmer's daughter, etc.*

This disgusted the Dodds sisters. In the same letter Norfolk says 'were' Bridlington and Jerves monasteries closed he 'should be at the suppressing, because the neighbouring country is populous and the houses greatly beloved by the people.'

Two days later, Norfolk commented to Cromwell about letters of Sir John, 'though perhaps he might say they were before the date of the pardon they show that no man had a more cankered heart'[46] and he continues, 'I think ye never read more lewd nor malicious letters.'[47] Sir John, Margaret, Ralph and others, though not the nobility, were to be tried at Westminster Hall on Wednesday 16 May 1537. 'Memoranda for prosecutions' state: 'Sir John Bulmer and his pretended wife were conspirators 'now of late' about Easter last, consented to Bigod's insurrection and plotted taking the Duke of Norfolk.' Ralph Bulmer, jun, wrote repeatedly since Xmas to his father persuading him to 'shift for himself.'[48] (Poor Margaret was at first sent to the wrong venue). Sir John was condemned by his own words and probably those of Staynhus, who seemingly 'turned King's evidence,'[49] as well as evidence from Ralph Bulmer, John Watts and Lord Lumley. Ralph was implicated by Sir John, and Margaret was condemned by Staynhus and Sir John. How could Sir John have betrayed the wife he idolised and his son? Well, the Dodds sisters are indulgent:

It is not just to blame Sir John too much. In his written confession he neither admitted his own guilt nor accused anyone else. But a weak-willed, impetuous man of his type must have been helpless under cross-examination against the will of his judges he persisted in calling Margaret his wife to the last.[50]

Margaret seems to have stood firm. There is a rather plaintive and sadly futile conclusion to Sir John's written statement, by the way. He spoke of buried treasure he knew of and the need for royal permission to search for it, continuing, 'If I had such authority I would charge the King nothing till it were found, and then let him reward me at his pleasure.'[51] (Lord Lumley succeeded in buying his freedom. Conversely, Thomas Neville reassured a woman regarding a clergyman, 'he shall not be put to death, for he hath no lands nor goods to lose.')[52]

Sir John and Margaret changed their pleas to guilty, perhaps in return for the pardoning of Ralph. The Dodds say Sir John's 'original crime was a natural reluctance to hand his nephew' Sir Francis Bigod 'over to the executioner.' Knowing this would be no defence, 'he was driven by terror and despair from plot to plot.'[53] Though Margaret had 'committed no overt act of treason; her offences, were merely words and silence' her 'irregular life' and lack of powerful support made her an easy 'example.' On Friday, 25 May 1537 the couple were parted for their execution. Sir John was hanged and beheaded at Tyburn and Margaret was burned at the stake at Smithfield. Also executed was the former Prior Cockerill. The Sunday before Margaret's execution Robert Jons complained of her fate to John Strebilhill, who replied, 'It is no pity, if she be a traitor to her prince, but that she should have after her deserving.' Jons then said, 'Let us speak no more of this matter, for men may be blamed for speaking the truth.' Jons was duly reported. The contemporary chronicler, Wriothesley, wrote of Margaret's execution: 'according to her judgement, God pardon her soul she was a very fair creature and a beautiful.'[54] And the execution of Sir John 'and the lady wife of Sir John Bomer' was referred to in a letter from 'R H (Robert Holdsworth), priest to Sir Henry Sayvel,' on 26 May 1537.[55] On 21 April 1537 Norfolk had written to Cromwell: 'Has caused indentures to be taken of' Sir John Bulmer's goods, which are of little value.'[56] This raises questions about Ralph Bulmer, heir to the estates, and, particularly, the young children of Sir John and Margaret. In addition to whatever arrangements the family made for them, these offspring did at least get regal sympathy. A Royal

Memorandum (dated only 1538) lists

> *Name of persons to be had at this time in the king's most benign remembrance: The widows and orphans of the persons attainted: Lord Husey's wife and children. Sir John Bulmer's children, sir Francis Bigod's wife and children, sir Thomas Percy's wife and children, sir Robert Constable's son, sir Stephen Hamerton's wife and children, Lord Darcy's son, Nicholas Tempest's wife and children, George Lomley's wife and children.*[57]

It is highly unlikely that the Bulmer orphans' uncle, Sir William, was in a position to take them in, judging by a comment from the time that he was 'always unthrifty. His wife and he have often lived asunder.'[58] The wife was 'Elizabeth, daughter and heire of William Elmeden of Elmeden and Tursdale.'[59] Problems between Sir William, who held a quarter of South Cowton manor according to Plantagenet Harrison's Bulmer pedigree, and his wealthy wife are further indicated by a letter of 27 February 1538, from Bishop Tunstall and John Uvedale (in Topclif) to the King:

> *On Saturday, 23rd February, sir William Bulmer, lately returned from London, repaired to his wife in county Durham, made search among the evidences of her inheritance and so departed unkindly from her, as is reported. She accordingly, on Sunday the 24th, made search, with a friar named Thomas Gibson and her servant William Asilbe, whether any of her evidences were embezzled, and found a letter (enclosed) written to sir William by the late revel sir John Bulmer all in his own hand, which as in duty bound she sent to us. Have charged the parties to keep the matter secret till your pleasure be known.*[60]

This may hint at weaknesses in Sir William's character; he does, though, seem to have been more cool and systematic than his brother, Sir John, as has been seen and also in his responses when being interrogated on 21 March (apparently 1538):

> *he did not read the letter to the end. This letter was brought to him to Wilton he left the said letter and all his other letters at Wilton, and Francis Bulmer, his son, took certain stuff and writings from Wilton, when the said Sir William was at London, and conveyed them to Sir William's house at Elmedenne, but whether he took the said letter among them Sir William knows not. Never showed the said letter or the effect thereof to any person. Never did anything for the fulfilment of any purpose contained in the said letter either in making beacons, setting watches, or otherwise. Never remembered the said letter, but*

laid it aside and forgot it.

Sir William also stated that he and Sir Ralph were asked 'to be counter sureties to the goodman of the Horse Head of Chepe, and to one Egglesfeld in Southwark.' regarding Ralph, then in the Tower. In the event Sir William did not need to be bound. (The interrogation record was 'In Ovedale's hand.')[61]

Notwithstanding Sir William's longer-term significance, Ralph was the heir. Imprisoned again, his name is carved (and fresh looking) inside Beauchamp Tower, from where he wrote to Sir Oswald Willestrop, asking for a loan and saying he was not afraid 'knows himself so clear that he doubts nothing of his short continuance in this your old lodging.' *The Fleet*, 6 May.[62] Ralph's statement on 23 April 1537 had spoken of the first phase of the uprising and he appears to have tried unsuccessfully to flee Cleveland by ship. Also, he and Uncle William warned that proclaiming of a letter at Guisborough would be plain treason. They were both forced to go with insurgents to Wilton and Sir John. He concluded: 'And I went into my mother's again and there did tarry and never stirred forth until St. Martin's Day.'[63] (Nov. 11th 1536) Whether the authorities were satisfied with this or whether a deal had been done with Sir John and Margaret subject to their changing their pleas to guilty, Ralph was pardoned. Seven years later, in May 1544, Ralph was knighted at Leith during a Scottish campaign. The following year 'Sir Ralph Bulmer'[64] was apparently a North Riding commissioner of the peace. (In 1540 one Joan Bulmer, wife of a possible relation of Ralph, was in the Royal Court, perhaps having blackmailed Queen Catherine for a position and who helped the Queen correspond with old flame, Francis Derham). The process continued with reference in 'The Pardon Rolls of 1547 to – Ralph Bulmer or Boulmer, the younger, Knight of London, alias, late of Wylton, Yorks, esquire;'[65] and rehabilitation was completed the following year when 'Sir Ralph Bulmer of Sutton in Holderness was restored in blood by *Act of Parliament*.'[66] It seems that Sir Ralph held the Bulmer and Wilton estates 'under a settlement by his grandfather Sir William' but in the case of Bulmer one Robert Bulmer, 'the bailiff', had a twenty one year lease from 1538, possibly in lieu of wages. Certainly the lands were lost to the family after Sir Ralph Bulmer's death on 9 October 1558. Wilton was described as being held by him in 'fee tail'[67] and Queen Mary immediately passed the manor to Sir Thomas Cornwallis and in 1583 the Fawethers purchased Bulmer from Queen Elizabeth. The will of Sir Ralph, who

Figure 5. The peaceful river Tees and Wilton Castle after rebuilding in about 1805.
Author's collection

had been a lawyer, was proved on 15 October. Amongst his bequests were: 'To John Bulmer' alias – 'John Cheyney, xx li. To everye of my servauntes three yeres wages.' And he was 'To be buried within the parish church of Sainte Botulphts without Bishopgate of London.'[68] He was survived by his daughters who were, with spouses names in brackets, – Joan (Francis Cholmely), Frances (Marmaduke Constable), Millicant (Thomas Grey), Dorothy (Ralph Williamson), Bridget (- Farley), Mary (- Morton) and Anne (Anthony Welbury and Gerard Lowther). And 'Complete Peerage' states, 'Among their representatives any hereditary Barony, that may be supposed to have been created in 1344, lost in 1537, and restored by implication in

1548, is in abeyance.' Sir Ralph's wife, Anne (Tempest), had died on 25 April 1555. Any marital happiness was short lived, as Sir Ralph would only accept 'the first three' daughters and they were the only ones referred to in the Inquisition post mortem and also the 1584 'Visitation pedigree.'[69]

Finally, a 'Grant of pardon of alienation to George Bowes knight,' etc., of 28 June 1580 refers to 'the manor of Little Busby, county York, and of lands there, late of Ralph Bulmer, deceased.'[70] The same year produced a lease related to ' lands' in Bulmer and Welburn, late of John Bulmer knight, attainted.'[71] Bulmer manor was apparently described about the time of forfeit as 'a very old house covered with slate and greatly in decay.'[72] Clearly the Lastingham home was given priority but Wilton Castle does not seem to have been neglected (Figures 5 and 6). Even in 1569 it was described as ifor Cleavland very servesable,'[73] though afterwards it deteriorated. There were signs of it around 1800 but there were none by 1846, though 'its ancient and venerable appearance' – was – 'well remembered by many of the inhabitants in the neighbourhood.'[74]

Figure 6. A rare sketch of Wilton Castle before restoration. *By permission of the British Library*

Conclusion

With Wilton lost and Sir Ralph's lack of a male heir, the fortunes of the Bulmers dwindled. Sir William's line continued with some prestige in County Durham but penalties for Catholicism, a ransom payment and fritterage led to their decline. The last Bulmer knight, the flamboyant Sir Bertram was buried at St Oswald's Durham in 1638. Like their Anglo-Viking ancestors, the Bulmer knights and Sheriffs are just a colourful memory. Yet the family's achievement in ensuring some native English continuity after the Norman Conquest, in a way, lives on.

In about 1805, Sir John Lowther built the present castle on the site of the old.

Notes and References

1. W Dickon Hoyle, G B Bulmer (ed) *Historical note of the Baronial House of Bulmer*, AD 1045-1750, p.91.
2. J Gardner, *Letters and Papers Foreign and Domestic of the Reign of Henry V111*, Eyre and Spottiswoode 1880s-1890s, vol V111, 1535 no 397.
3. *Monastic Chancery Proceedings* 1533-39, quotes supplied by Hutton le Hole local historian Mr R H Hayes.
4. University of Leeds, Extraction from *Yorks Star Chambers Proceedings*, Yorkshire Archaeological Society Record Server vol 41 no 30, pp.63-72.
5. Gardner, *op cit.* vol X11, 1537, part II, item 189.
6. R W Hoyle, *The Pilgrimage of Grace and the Politics of the 1530s*, Oxford University Press, 2001, p.397.
7. M H and R Dodds, *The Pilgrimage of Grace*, 1536-7, and *The Exeter Conspiracy*, 1538, Cambridge University Press (1915) vol I, p.39.
8. Dodds, *ibid*, p39.
9. The Hon Vicary Gibbs (ed) *The Complete Peerage of England Scotland Ireland Great Britain and the United Kingdom extant extinct or dormant*, GEC New Edition vol II, p.419.
10. John Walker Ord, *The History and Antiquities of Cleveland*, Simpkin and Marshall (1846) republished by Patrick and Shotton (1972) p386.
11. Dodds, *op cit* vol I, p39.
12. Hobson Bulmer MA, *Bulmer Family Chronicle*, before 1050-1936, (1937) p107.
13. Gardner, *op cit* vol III, 1535, no 1024.
14. P Williams, *The Pilgrimage of Grace*, article in Purnell's *History of the English Speaking People*, magazine no 36.
15. A Fletcher, *Tudor Rebellions*, Longmans (1968) *Letters and papers of Henry VIII* XI 705 (4), p122.
16. Dodds, *op cit* vol I, p20.
17. University of Leeds, *Letters and Papers of Henry VIII*, extracts.
18. Gardner, *op cit* vol XI, 1536, no 129 Leeds University.
19. Dodds, *op cit* vol II, p50.
20. Gardner, *op cit* vol XII, 1537, part 1 no 66, *op cit* vol II, p52.
21. Gardner, *op cit* vol XII, 1537, part 1 no 164.
22. Gardner, *ibid* no 1083.
23. Gardner, *ibid* no 236, University of Leeds, *op cit Letters and Papers of Henry VIII*, extracts.
24. Gardner, *op cit.*
25. Dodds, *op cit* vol II, p96.
26. Dodds, *ibid* p97.
27. Gardner, *op cit* vol XII, 1537, part I, item 1083
28. Dodds, *op cit* vol II, p158.
29. Dodds, *ibid* pp 158-9.

30. Dodds, *ibid* p159.
31. Dodds, *ibid* p158.
32. Dodds, *ibid* p159.
33. Dodds, *ibid* p159.
34. Dodds, *ibid* p 161.
35. Dodds, *ibid* p162.
36. Dodds, *ibid* p163.
37. Dodds, *ibid* p160.
38. M H and R Dodds, *ibid* p159.
39. Gardner, *op cit* vol XII, 1537, part 1 no 1083.
40. Gardner, *ibid* vol XII, 1537, part 1 no 9.
41. Tower of London Records.
42. Public Record Office, *Letters and Papers of Foreign and Domestic*, 29 Henry VIII 1039.
43. University of Leeds, *op cit* transcript no 33.
44. Tower of London Records.
45. Dodds, *op cit* vol II, p135.
46. Gardner, *ibid* vol XII, 1537, part I no 1184.
47. Dodds, *op cit* vol II p201.
48. Gardner, *op cit* vol XII, 1537, part I no 1088.
49. Dodds, *op cit* vol II p200.
50. Dodds, *ibid* vol II pp201-2.
51. Public Record Office, document SP1/119.
52. Dodds, *op cit* vol II p185.
53. Dodds, *ibid* p201.
54. M H and R Dodds, *ibid* pp215-6.
55. Gardner, *op cit* vol XII, 1537, part I no 1285.
56. Gardner, *ibid* no 991.
57. British Library Department of Manuscripts, *Royal Memoranda*.
58. Gardner, *op cit* vol XIII, 1538, part I.
59. Surtees, *History and Antiquities of the County Palatine of Durham*, vol I (1816) p79.
60. Public Records Office, *Letters and Papers Foreign and Domestic* 29 Henry VIII 365.
61. Gardner, *op cit* vol XIII, 1538, part I.
62. Public Record Office Document SP1/119.
63. University of Leeds, *op cit Letters and Papers of Henry VIII* no 7.
64. Public Record Office, Patent Roll 17 Henry VIII.
65. M A Hobson Bulmer, *op cit* p121.
66. The Hon Vicary Gibbs, *op cit* vol II p419.
67. W Page (ed) *Victorian History of the County of York North Riding*, vol II pp48 and 109-10, St Cuthbert's Press (1923).
68. The publications of the Surtees Society, *North Country Wills*, vol CXXI P7 (1912).
69. The Hon Vicary Gibbs, *op cit* pp419-20.
70. Public Record Office, Patent Roll 22 Elizabeth XII m10.
71. Public Record Office, Patent Roll 22 Elizabeth IV mm 15-16.
72. Public Record Office, Letters and Papers Foreign and Domestic 29 Henry VIII 44.
73. W Page, *op cit* vol II p374.
74. John Walker Ord, *op cit* p389.

General Reading
John Guy, *Tudor England*, Oxford University Press (1988).
Allison Weir and Jonathan Cape, *Henry VIII King and Court*, (2001).

Acknowledgements

To Anne Williams and Paul Bolton, historians of the post-Conquest period for their help with the origins of the Bulmers.

13. MOCK MAYORS OF MIDDLETON

by Paul Screeton

THE TRADITION OF 'MOCK MAYORS' is one of folklore's lesser-known and least explored outposts. Possibly the only remaining example exists in the tiny community of Middleton in Hartlepool centred upon the Smallcrafts Club that is hidden away from the touristy commercialisation of the burgeoning marina.

Mock mayors in days of yore were generally elected as the greatest drunkard or derelict in the community. It was a deliberate demonstration by nonconformists of putting two fingers up at authority.

A Spontaneous Tradition

The Middleton mayoralty is only quite recent in its inception, but it derives from a noble and ancient tradition. It is probably unique in the twenty first century. It is also special in that its genesis was wholly spontaneous.

The notion of electing a mayor in Middleton came about without prior knowledge of the historical antecedents of such an unofficial office.

Middletonians lived in smart cabins (some having been there for sixty years) by the harbour and they socialized in the Smallcrafts Club. Their very existence and rights were often under threat, so they had banded together and were led by what was known as the Banks Top Committee.

It was the trusty triumvirate of trade union official Owen Richmond, engineer George 'Geordie' Grainger and coal merchant Bertie Cox who sparked the idea of having their own local mayor.

Owen Richmond was the first to hold office in 1970, and was particularly proud to hold the title again in 1982, as it was also Maritime England Year. In all, he has held the post of mayor four times (Figure 1). Of the inaugurators of the honour, Bertie Cox was installed in 1971 and George Grainger held the title in 1975, 1978 and 1979.

Spirit of Middleton

The first Middleton chain of office followed the tradition of mocking

Figure 1. Owen Richmond, four times Mayor of Middleton. *Author's collection*

authority by being formed by two lavatory chains being attached to a Durham Light Infantry shield. The current chain is more presentable and has a special coat of arms with a proud emblem (Figure 2).

Between the townships of the ancient borough of Hartlepool and the upstart West Hartlepool there was a marshy area known as The Slake. Long before a road, harbours and shipbuilders' yards were created, each summer, around July, a large flock of herons would roost every night on this stretch of mudflats. Apparently the Middletonians – there were then several rows of houses and a handful of public houses – became so attached to this migratory occurrence that they adopted the birds as an emblem. Perhaps the herons followed the shoals of herring from Scotland to the Thames, stopping off awhile at The Slake. Whatever, the bird is honoured on

Figure 2. The present impressive badge of office. *Owen Richmond*

the chain of office by the ancestors of the Middleton residents who took the graceful fishing birds to their bosom.

Many mourned the demolition of the housing in Middleton, leaving, as its only reminder, the Smallcrafts Club. Long distance lorry driver Jackie Knight, mayor in 1988, commented at the time:

We can't preserve the community, the people were moved out, but we can preserve the spirit of Middleton, that is very much alive. I think that will give you some idea why it is so important to have a mayor and honour tradition.

A Mocking of Mayors

Doubtless somewhere there is a collective noun for mayors, but here I'll mention just a few of Middleton's first citizens.

Owen Richmond, who retired in 1988 as district secretary of the Amalgamated Union of Engineering Workers, encapsulates the spirit of Middleton. He is a man of some guile and one year saved the harbour fete by his cunning machinations. He has also been prominent in the fight to retain a right of way through the docks. In addition he has campaigned for a general clean up of the area and against the licensed sea-coal dredger, which he argued changed the beaches for the worst.

In 1987, Sandra Steel became the first lady to be so honoured, striking a blow for women's lib. The Furness Street woman was a leading member of the Smallcrafts Club and a tireless fundraiser for charity. Her husband Les is the club's steward.

The mayor elected in 1981 was Alex Weegram, then working in the *Hartlepool Mail's* pressroom. Born into a family of eleven in Middleton in 1922, his father was a dock pilot. At fourteen he joined the *Cameratta* as a galley boy and ended up sailing all over the world. During the Second World War, he served in convoys and later worked on a dredger at Hartlepool before becoming a diver.

The current mayor is octogenarian Jimmy Hall, who was born in Slake Terrace. He was brought up in Middleton with Teddy Gardner who went on to hold British Empire and European Flyweight boxing titles. Jimmy has plenty of tales about his war exploits, including how his vessel lifted a sunken German ship where they found medals struck to celebrate an Axis power victory by Germany and Italy, The eighty-two year old remorsefully recalls that he didn't have the sense to keep a few to sell. After France capitulated he returned to Hartlepool, where he enlisted on locally built ship *Candida* along with other local men, and on her he served for another four years, going to Canada and the Mediterranean. Subsequently he worked for Clarence Erection, maintaining equipment in various North East pits.

Mayor's Parlour

The Mayor of Middleton's parlour is the Smallcrafts Club in

Figure 3. The mayoral parlour, the interior of the Smallcrafts Club. *Harry Harland courtesy of the Hartlepool Mail*

Commercial Street (Figure 3). While the marina developers have created a new world vision, the Smallcrafts is the embarrassing old world reality-where Small is really beautiful.

The Smallcrafts Association started life in a cottage owned by the father of the renowned boxer, Teddy Gardner. After searching for suitable premises, the organisation came across the then Prince of Wales public house, which was rented out to them by Cameron's Brewery (they even donated a barrel of beer to kick the group off in fine style.) Over the decades, the members worked hard not only on repairs to their clubhouse, which they were eventually able to lease after lengthy negotiations with the Teesside Development

Corporation, but to raise cash for numerous charities.

Here people with a love of the sea swap yarns, have a few beers and play pool or darts.

A New Century

The annual ceremony got off to a bad start in 2001, with a couple of embarrassing hiccups when the traditional Easter mayor making was missed. The women's committee, which apparently was supposed to organize the event, was blamed for the oversight; I myself urged that the ceremony must still take place even if a little late. On the rearranged Bank Holiday Monday, planned recipient Jimmy Hall failed to appear, not knowing that it was his big day, the choice being kept a closely guarded secret. Owen Richmond finally did the honours by placing the chain of office round Jimmy's neck on a later day of my choice (Figure 4). Owen the made a brief speech, and afterwards said that Jimmy was chosen because he's a grand chap and probably the only person in the association alive who was actually born in Middleton.

The mayoralty was saved, but in 1999 the forty-eight cabins were moved from their original site to another quieter spot with a splendid

Figure 4. Jimmy Hall being inaugurated as mayor by Owen Richmond. *Author's collection*

view over the bay. Everyone seemed quite happy with the re-encampment.

A National Phenomenon

My fascination for the Mayors of Middleton put me in touch with a retired polytechnic lecturer and fellow student of mock mayors, Derek Froome. I have him to thank for summarizing material he has collected from the North East.

Durham City had its Duke of Baubleshire, a character who was ennobled as a tribute to his eccentricity. Newcastle Boys' Grammar School often elected a boy mayor. At Embelton, Northumberland, there was a regular election of a tramp or other derelict as mayor after having been made drunk, the local vicar had the tradition put down. Also in Ford, Northumberland there was an annual election of a drunken mayor. In Victorian times, the custom was often met by hostility from the clergy or police. The Mayor of Middleton was new to Derek and he wrote to me 'Mock mayors are very fugitive and their discovery is more often than not a pursuit of serendipity'.

Fellow folklorist Peter Christie has researched the mock mayors of his native North Devon. He has found seven spoofs of the real thing, where election days seem to have been an excuse for a holiday spent in drinking and making speeches attacking real or perceived abuses of power by local councils and the government. During the nineteenth century he found references to these functionaries at Bideford, Parracombe (where by tradition the mayor was pushed around in a wheelbarrow and tipped into the mill pond at the end of the day) Torrington, Chittlehampton, Buckland Brewer (the nomination going to the most notorious wife-beater in the village) Derby and Bradiford (both suburbs of Barnstaple).

The Mayor of Derby showed the office was not just humorous by writing letters to the press calling for work to be carried out to improve the roads and drainage in his area. He even went so far as to lead a crowd, with an attendant band, in a mass trespass along a disputed footpath to Landkey. In an echo of this 1840s political act, Smallcrafts (Figure 5) activist Owen Richmond led a similar illegal protest against Tees and Hartlepool Port Authority's to bar walkers from a disputed right-of-way across Hartlepool Docks.

Postscript

The First World War probably put paid to these ancient traditions and as I have suggested, Middleton's mayors are probably unique in the twenty first century. It would be remiss of me if I did not

Figure 5. The unprepossessing exterior of the Smallcrafts Club where ancient tradition lives on. *Author's collection*

acknowledge there might be some semblance of other continuing recent traditions.

The host of the television quiz show *Countdown*, Richard Whiteley, joked on air that he would like to be Mayor of Wetwang, in the heart of the Wolds in East Yorkshire, and villagers took him up on his offer at a ceremony in June 1988. It's a post, I believe, he still holds and he is part owner of a racehorse called *Mayor of Wetwang*.

As seen, mock mayors have been selected in the past from the less salubrious section of society. The *Sun* newspaper, sometime in 1991, had a single paragraph announcing that eighteen-year-old builder Fevin Oatley is an idiot-officially-clinching the village idiot title in Croscombe, Somerset.

Lastly, a 1999 international news snippet reported that the townsfolk of Porto Alegre, Brazil, were fed up with their local politicians and decided to teach them a lesson. For a joke, they nominated a pig in the town's elections, but the joke backfired when the animal was elected after polling 2,573 votes.

As I write this, the public of Hartlepool has voted narrowly to choose a high-profile town mayor along the lines of New York and London, against the advice of all three political parties on the council. Shades of the mock mayor tradition of power to the people!

Appendix: A Mayoral Chronology:

1970 Owen Richmond	1982 Owen Richmond	1994 Derek Gordon Douglas
1971 Bertie Cox	1983 Peter Dawson	1995 Elizabeth Reeve
1972 Winston Pearson	1984 Winston Pearson	1996 Frederick Wales
1973 Jimmy Hall	1985 Leslie Hall	1997 Mary Moon
1974 Owen Richmond	1986 Vic Felgate	1998 Annette Tighe
1975 George Grainger	1987 Sandra Steel	2000 Brian Horsley
1976 Owen Richmond	1988 Jackie Knight	2001 Jimmy Hall
1977 Jimmy Hall	1989 Jack O'Grady	
1978 George Grainger	1990 Billy Gilfoyle	
1979 George Grainger	1991 Les Steel	
1980 Owen Richmond	1992 Billy Winspear	
1981 Alex Weegram	1993 Barney Walls	

THE EDITOR

Maureen Anderson was born in Scotland in 1948 and moved with her family to Australia whilst still a child. On returning to Britain in the early 1970s, she lived in Wetherby, West Yorkshire for two years then moved to Seaton Carew where she still lives. Her mother, a keen member of the National Trust, brought her up to have a love of antiques and history. On moving to Seaton she researched the history of the village and wrote her first book and has since written other books on the area. She has recently researched an archive of photographs for Bowes Museum, taken of Seaton Carew between 1885 and 1890; these will be available on the internet in 2002.

CONTRIBUTORS

1. 'TEESSIDE': A CURIOUS JOURNEY

Tom Pailor, born in Hartlepool in 1939, acquired a strong interest in local politics from his father, Thomas Henry Pailor, who served on the old Borough Council of Hartlepool for over twenty years. Following an undistinguished school career at Rosebank High School, Tom left in 1956 with, it must be said, a love of the English language courtesy of his English teacher, Mr Hetherington. Joining his family's business on their 100th anniversary, Tom served a traditional engineering apprenticeship as a turner and during his forty-five years was responsible for J J Hardy's relocation to their current site and the transformation from traditional brass

foundry into one of the UK's premier CNC machine shops, specialising in the supply of equipment to the United Kingdom's transportation industries. Now retired from day-to-day affairs at the family business, this article has been written as one of Tom's first retirement projects and he would like to thank Madge for her typing and advice, Ray for all the books and research, and Thel for the idea. His major interests are skiing (badly), cycling slowly and following Leeds United. He is also a keen gardener and Rotarian.

2. A BIG DAY OUT AT PORT DARLINGTON

Norman Moorsom was born in Middlesbrough and educated at Middlesbrough Boys' High School and St John's College of Education in York. He taught for ten years in comprehensive schools around Middlesbrough, and was then appointed as Museum Schools Service Officer for the County Borough of Teesside, a post he held for over sixteen years. He then became Local History Officer for Cleveland County Council, taking early retirement in 1993. Since 1963, Norman has written thirty-five booklets and books about the Middlesbrough area. He enjoys giving lectures on local history, as well as taking guided walks around the area of the original town. He is a founder member of the Cleveland and Teesside Local History Society, established in 1968, and chairman of Middlesbrough Heritage Group. He met his wife, Sylvia when she was Senior Assistant at Middlesbrough Reference Library where much of his early research took place. They have a son, Richard, a daughter, Hilary, and two grandchildren, Laura and Andrew.

3. WHAT'S IN A NAME?

Simon Chapman has lived for most of his life in Brotton, a village in the centre of what was once the most productive iron ore-mining field in Britain. Whilst still at school he became aware of the void left in his home area by the closure of the last mine in January 1964 and began to talk to former ironstone miners about their work. He visited local mining sites and began to record their physical remains by taking photographs and preparing measured drawings. Later he began to undertake research and to date has written about a dozen books and several articles about Cleveland ironstone mining. In 2000 he took early retirement after thirty-two years as a cartographic surveyor in the Ordnance Survey, and in future intends to carry on researching and recording industrial archaeology with the support of his wife, Clare.

4. THE WRECK OF THE 'BIRGER'

Gary Green was born in Easington, County Durham on 7 February 1959. He has spent his life in the seaside resort of Redcar, just a few miles from the mouth of the river Tees. Growing up less than a hundred yards from the Redcar Rocks, it is no surprise that they became his natural 'playground' and his parents resigned themselves to the fact that he would come home at night with wet feet! Educated first at Zetland Primary School and then Sir William Turner's Boy's Grammar School, it was here that he became captivated by the Jacques
Cousteau programmes on television. At fifteen his father enrolled him in the local branch of the British Sub-Aqua Club. There he met Jimmy Dick, little realising that twenty years on they would discover the wreck of the *Birger*. His interest in shipwrecks grew and he began collecting and still does to this day, charts, maps, books and newspaper cuttings. He spent a number of years as an Engineer Officer for the Blue Star Line of Liverpool and then settled ashore and resumed diving, joining the Cleveland Divers of which he is still a member. Now, married to Claire, he is employed by Tees Archaeology where he specialises in maritime archaeology.

5. MONKEY BUSINESS: NOT AT ALL NAPOLEONIC
13. MOCK MAYORS OF MIDDLETON

Paul Screeton was born in Hartlepool in 1945 and he and his wife live in Seaton Carew. He spent thirty-five years as a journalist before taking early retirement. He has had a number of books published on folklore, earth mysteries and the paranormal. In addition to writing as a freelance for a number of publications, he edits a magazine devoted to urban belief tales.

6. LOOKING BACK IN TIME

Brian Arnison was born in 1945 at West Hartlepool. He married Patricia Ryan and they have two children, Ian and Elizabeth. He was educated at Dyke House Secondary Modern School and on leaving was apprenticed as a bookbinder to M A Windross of F W Mason, Printers and Bookbinders. He studied bookbinding and warehouse work at the College of Art and Industrial Design, Newcastle-upon-Tyne and the London School of Printing. He worked at Sangorski & Suttcliffe of London, one of the best bookbinders in the world. When he returned to Hartlepool in 1970 there was no employment for his craft so he worked as a Quality Control Inspector in the steel industry. Now living in Seaton Carew, he has spent the last twenty-five years inspecting at plate and pipe mills all over the world.

7. ZEPPELIN LISTENING POSTS

John W Perrin originated from Surrey, moving to Hartlepool in 1967. He has always had a keen interest in aviation history. He served in the RAF for three years and later, in a spare time capacity, joined the Royal Observer Corps, completing his service as a Group Officer when the organisation stood down in 1992. He is now a chairman of the ROC Northern Area Collection, with an exhibition of corps history at the North East Aircraft Museum in Sunderland. His wife Olivia, who took the accompanying photographs, is a professional photographer.

8. River Tees: Lifeblood of the Tees Valley
10. Stockton Castle: Gone and Almost Forgotten

Robert Woodhouse, born in Rotherham, South Yorkshire, spent his early years there before a family move to Middlesbrough where he attended Acklam Hall Grammar School from 1957-1964. A teacher training course and BA (Hons) degree in history from the University of London led to a teaching career spanning almost thirty years in Middlesbrough, Rotherham, Darlington and Stockton-on-Tees. He began researching and writing on aspects of local history in the 1960s and since then has seen the publication of eighteen  books as well as regular contributions to local radio and newspapers (these include a weekly walks column spanning ten years for the *Middlesbrough Evening Gazette*). He now runs adult education courses on North East history and lectures to groups and societies in the area.

9. Monks, Money and Middlesbrough

Geoff S Braddy is a former history teacher from Middlesbrough. He was educated locally and studied history at the University of Leeds. He has been secretary of the Cleveland and Teesside Local History Society for several years and has contributed to a number of books on local history as well as writing for *Cleveland History* and other journals. His special interest is Cleveland in the middle ages.

11. CLEVELAND CHEMICAL INDUSTRY

David Tomlin B Sc, as an industrial chemist, came to live and work in the area some thirty-six years ago. He has worked for both ICI at Billingham and British Steel Research at Grangetown. He was a former secretary and is now committee member of the Cleveland Industrial Archaeology Society. He is also a member of the Cleveland and Teesside Local History Society and works on the management committee of the Tom Leonard Mining Museum at Skinningrove. In 2000, he founded the organisation Friends of Teesside Archives. Currently he serves the ward of Normanby as a Councillor on Redcar and Cleveland Borough Council.

12. VIKING DESCENT: THE BULMERS OF WILTON-IN-CLEVELAND CASTLE

Peter Davison was born in Liverpool of north-eastern parents. He is a teacher of history, English and German and has taught on exchange in Denmark. Previously he worked as a policeman in York and Scarborough. His interests include boating at Runswick Bay, hiking on the North Yorkshire Moors, going to the cinema and listening to live bands in the local and concert theatres. His parental grandmother was a Bulmer and family legend connects her with the Bulmer barons.

INDEX

Places

Other places